Success with Mathematics

Many students find the leap between school and university-level mathematics to be significantly greater than they expected. *Success with Mathematics* has been devised and written especially in order to help students bridge that gap. It offers clear, practical guidance from experienced teachers of mathematics in higher education on such key issues as:

- Getting ready
- Ways of studying
- Assessment
- Mathematical communication
- Learning by doing
- Using ICT when studying mathematics
- Using calculators
- Preparing for examinations and resources

After reading this book, students will find themselves much better prepared for the change in pace, rigour and abstraction they encounter in university mathematics. They will also find themselves able to broaden their learning strategies and improve their self-directed study skills. This book is essential reading for anyone following, or about to undertake, a degree in mathematics, or other degree courses with mathematical content.

Heather Cooke is Academic Liaison Officer with the Centre for Mathematics Education at The Open University.

This book has been written by experienced Open University lecturers and tutors with a great deal of help from colleagues in other universities – and from students. The tasks and advice offered here are based on considerable experience of working with adults, both young and mature, many of whom initially had limited self-study skills and low confidence in their ability to learn mathematics.

Contributing authors:
Barbara Allen
Julia Burnell
Heather Cooke (Course Chair)
Sally Crighton
Sue Johnston-Wilder
Liam McCloskey
John Mason
June Parker
Mike Underhill
Richard Walker

Faculty steering group:
Gaynor Arrowsmith
Judith Daniels
Judy Ekins
Judy Emms
Jeremy Gray
Ian Harrison
Phil Rippon
Mike Simpson

Academic editor:
David Pimm

External assessor:
David Driffel

Course manager:
Maggie Jenkins

Research assistant:
Hilary Evens

Critical readers:
Gaynor Arrowsmith
Jenny Houssart
Joe Kyle
Douglas Quinney
Frank van der Molen

If you would like to find out about available OU courses, please write for the prospectus to the Call Centre, PO Box 724, The Open University, Walton Hall, Milton Keynes MK7 6ZW, UK (telephone + 44 1908 653231).

The web page http://mcs.open.ac.uk/SkillMath/ supports this book and has links to The Open University web site and the Mathematics and Computing Faculty Maths Choices page.

Success with Mathematics

Heather Cooke

Routledge
Taylor & Francis Group

LONDON AND NEW YORK

Centre for
Mathematics
Education

The Open
University

First published 2003 by Routledge
11 New Fetter Lane, London EC4P 4EE

Simultaneously published in the USA and Canada
by Routledge
29 West 35th Street, New York, NY 10001

Routledge is an imprint of the Taylor & Francis Group

© 2003 The Open University

Typeset in Goudy by Wearset Ltd, Boldon, Tyne and Wear
Printed and bound in Great Britain by MPG Books Ltd, Bodmin

British Library Cataloguing in Publication Data
A catalogue record for this book is available from the British Library

Library of Congress Cataloging in Publication Data
A catalog record has been requested

ISBN 0-415-29860-1 (hbk)
ISBN 0-415-29861-X (pbk)

Contents

1 Introduction – read this first!   1
Learning mathematics   1
    Active learning   1
    When and how to use this book   2
Mathematics at university   3
    Topics in mathematics   3
How to use this book   5
    Possible outcomes from using this book   5

2 Getting ready   7
First steps   7
    What is studying about?   8
    Why study mathematics?   8
    Keys to effective study   11
Finding and managing time   11
    Using each study session effectively   13
Getting the right resources organised   14
    Study setting   14
    Equipment   15
    Other resources   17
Looking after people   18
    Yourself   18
    Family, friends, colleagues and teaching staff   19
Reflection   20

3 Ways of studying   22
The diversity of study   22
    Using different modes of study   23
    Study skills   24
Studying on your own   24

Learning with other people   25
  Lectures   26
  Self-help groups   29
Making and keeping notes   29
  Lecture notes   29
  Notes from study modules   30
  Notes from textbooks   31
  Notes from non-written sources   33
  Other types of notes   33
Learning through reading   35
  Course units   35
  Textbooks   37
Reflection   40

4 Assessment   **42**
About assessment   42
  How courses are formally assessed   43
Continuous assessment   43
  What are assignments for?   43
  Types of formal assessment   44
  Planning and doing assignments   46
  Looking ahead   47
  Working on individual questions   48
  You are not alone   50
  Putting your assignment together   51
  All about marks   53
  What to do when you get your assignment back   56
  Keep going   58
Examinations   58
  Why examinations are necessary   58
  Planning your revision   59
  Revision resources   62
  Revision techniques   62
  Preparing for the examination   68
  Doing the examination   72
  After the examination   74

5 Mathematical communication   **76**
Representing mathematics   76
Reading and speaking mathematics   80
  Reading about mathematics   80
  Talking about mathematics   82
  Making a presentation   83
Writing mathematics   84
  To type or not to type?   87

Contents

Diagrams and graphs	88
Diagrams	88
Graphs	89
Graphing mathematical functions	91
Plotting coordinates	91
Plotting functions	92
Sketching functions	93
Reflection	97
6 Learning by doing	**98**
Introduction	98
Mental powers	99
Imagining and expressing	99
Specialising and generalising	102
Conjecturing and convincing	106
Organising and characterising	107
Mathematical themes	112
Doing and undoing	112
Invariance amidst change	113
Extending and contracting meaning	113
Freedom and constraint	114
Learning by communicating	114
Understanding mathematics	116
Expressing yourself mathematically	117
Convincing as a process	117
Reflection	119
7 Using ICT when studying mathematics	**122**
What is available	122
Information	124
The Internet	124
Communication	125
Electronic	125
Written	126
Computation	131
Computer algebra systems	132
Data handling	134
Databases and spreadsheets	134
Data logging	134
Learning	136
Role of technology	137
Tutor	137
Tools	138
Tutee	141
How does technology affect a problem?	142
Reflection	144

8 Using calculators   **145**
   Types of calculator   145
      What is available?   146
      Scientific calculators   147
      Buying your own calculator   148
   Getting to know your calculator   149
      To use or not to use your calculator ...   149
      Limitations   150
      Key keys   151
      Constants and memory   154
      Rounding   155
      To infinity and beyond ...   156
      Fractions   157
      Reciprocals   157
      Angles   157
      Trigonometry   159
      Random numbers   160
      Easy counting!   160

9 What next?   **164**
   Introduction   164
   Domestic preparation   165
   Academic preparation   166
      Mathematics   166
      Background reading   167
   Resources   167
      Mathematics revision   167
      Mathematics reference   167
      Wider mathematical reading   168
      Study skills   169

Index   **170**

1

Introduction – read this first!

This book is intended for people taking courses involving some mathematics. It is aimed at students in higher education, but it is also relevant for those working towards A level. How much of the book is relevant to you, and when you should use it, will depend on your own circumstances. You may just be getting used to organising your own study, perhaps have not studied for a long time, or may not feel very confident about your ability to learn mathematics – or all three.

LEARNING MATHEMATICS

Learning mathematics is not just about acquiring and mastering computational and problem-solving techniques, or solely about understanding definitions, arguments and proofs, or even simply about knowing how to work with examples and counter-examples. In addition to all of these things, it also involves you reconstructing the thinking and work of other mathematicians, so that it becomes part of your own thinking, as well as you undertaking your own mathematical activity and exploration. Learning mathematics requires you to develop ways of thinking mathematically while doing mathematics – for many, the most exciting and creative element of all.

Active learning

This is not the usual kind of textbook. For a start, it is designed for people working on their own rather than in a class setting. It is possible to learn quite a lot just by reading it, but for more effective, long-term learning, it is best to be actively engaged as well. This includes trying things out for yourself, making notes and talking to other people about what you have read (and possibly re-read, for seldom can one reading be enough to gain a good understanding when mathematics is involved). To help you get into this possibly less familiar mode of learning, there are numerous tasks for you to do throughout this book: most have comments or solutions immediately following. You are strongly advised to try each task for yourself before looking at the Comment, so if your eyes tend to read on, you may need to develop a means of masking these comments initially – especially for the more mathematical tasks.

Task 1.1 Getting an overview

Read quickly through the contents pages, in order to get an overview of what is in the book. Then flick through the book as a whole to get a feel for what is in it and how it is organised, glancing at the general layout of the chapters. You can get an idea of the type of content by skimming over the headings and subheadings, without reading anything in detail.

Comment
These are some of the things you might have noticed.

There are more words than you might have expected in a book about mathematics. The book is written in nine chapters that have headings and subheadings. There are tasks, with comments immediately afterwards, and also notes in boxes. There are different types of diagrams, graphs and tables. The contents page lists the chapters and main sections within them and there is an index at the back.

When and how to use this book

The book is designed to help you prepare for studying mathematics at university level, but there are sections that will also be of help once you have embarked on your course. Things you may not think are important as you prepare may become more significant as you get into your course. So the book is not only for preparation but also for support while you study.

It may be a long time since you studied, so you may not be very confident or that sure about your current mathematical skill or your ability to learn mathematics. If this is the case, then start at Chapter 2 and work your way through the book from the beginning. But if you are feeling confident as a student responsible for your own learning, then it may be more appropriate for you to dip into different sections, for example Chapter 6, Learning by doing. The book can be drawn on in a variety of ways – it is yours, so use it in ways that help *you*.

Like any other, this book is unlikely to cover everything you need. It is primarily about *how* to study mathematics rather than providing you with an in-depth discussion of specific mathematical ideas and techniques. Nevertheless, it should support you in developing sufficient skill and confidence to be able to use other resources. (Some such resources are listed in Chapter 9.)

MATHEMATICS AT UNIVERSITY

What has your relationship been with mathematics up to now, and how would you assess your current relationship?

Task 1.2 What sort of student are you?

Which of the following most closely matches your current situation?

- Mathematics pops up in the most unexpected places. I thought I wouldn't need it for my course, but there it was, in disguise.
- I have always been reasonably good at mathematics and would like to study it further, but do not have that much confidence, especially recognising where to start with a solution.
- I love mathematics and want to find out the most effective ways of working and strategies for coping when I get stuck.
- I used to find mathematics easy, but have had a year or so away from studying it and can't really remember a lot.
- I have always found mathematics hard to understand, but I need it for my job.

Comment
Your experiences of mathematics may differ from these mathematical learners, but basically the book offers some guidance on what to expect and how to proceed, no matter which of these individuals you feel closest to. Read the details of your course carefully and be prepared to ask for more information. Access and foundation courses, available at some universities, can also be used to bring your mathematical background and understanding up to the required level.

Topics in mathematics

It is perhaps helpful to see mathematics as a combination of what has been developed: (i) because of the need for solving particular, real-world problems and (ii) as the result of a more general and abstract search for and exploration of patterns and relationships; leading to the development of various ways of expressing and justifying them. These two aspects can be thought of as: (i) mathematics as a toolkit deployed for other human tasks and (ii) mathematics as a discipline and means of enquiry in its own right. What is taught at school is a mix of topics and approaches from this rich and complex tapestry, which has arisen from human engagement with mathematics for nearly 5000 years.

Lower-school mathematics mainly concentrates on the concrete operations and techniques for calculating. More abstract concepts and means are gradually introduced, such as ratio and proportion, algebraic manipulation and transformation in a variety of guises. A learner of mathematics has to become proficient at applying rules and techniques that mathematicians have developed over the years.

On the whole, universities are restricted in what is taken as prior knowledge by the nature of the upper-school mathematics curriculum. Although modules can additionally be taken in statistics, mechanics and discrete (decision) mathematics at school, the compulsory core units tend to be in the topics of pure mathematics and most university mathematics departments now make no assumption about non-core material.

What do universities expect?
This differs from university to university and certainly from course to course. For those courses with little overt mathematical elements (mathematics seen primarily as a toolkit), for example quantitative methods, the assumption is likely to be GCSE grade C, with some facility at re-arranging formulae being particularly useful. For programmes that specify A-level, most universities assume no other knowledge than the compulsory elements of the A-level syllabus. However, you are expected to be pretty fluent in your use and understanding of these elements, particularly algebraic processes and the nature of proof. Most mathematics departments would also expect that if you are studying mathematics as a discipline in its own right, you will have read some books and thought about the nature of mathematics. (Some examples of this growing literature *about* mathematics are listed at the end of Chapter 9.)

Here are some extracts from 2001 prospectuses for BSc mathematics degrees.

> There is a basic 'tool kit' which every Mathematics undergraduate needs to master – such tools belong mainly to the realm of Pure Mathematics.
>
> (University of Leicester)

> At first the Mathematics course has considerable overlap with A-level.
>
> (University of Durham)

However, there are a few university courses and modules that do not assume A-level mathematics. For example:

> If you have less mathematical background or would like a course to build up skills and knowledge at a slower pace, consider MU120

Open Mathematics, even if you are currently contemplating taking further courses in mathematics.

(The Open University)

Universities include a variety of topics in their first-year mathematics courses, so check with your university by looking in their prospectus, phoning for details or visiting their web site. Details of all UK university courses are available through the University and College Advisory Service (UCAS) directory, which can be accessed via the UCAS web site (http://www.ucas.ac.uk). A common prerequisite for all courses is to be proficient in the use of algebraic techniques.

What should you expect?
This book goes into some detail about what to expect and provides advice on how to deal with university study. It makes suggestions that should help with pacing yourself, so that you do not get hopelessly behind, and it details different methods of learning at university, as well as describing some strategies to help with retention. Universities recognise that it is normal for students to get stuck or be unable to understand. Believe it or not, this is an essential stage in learning mathematics (and is discussed further in Chapter 6).

HOW TO USE THIS BOOK

This is not a book to read passively through from cover to cover. You may choose to work through it in order, doing each task as it arises. But there are many other ways it might be used, so it can help to be clear about what you want or need to get from using it – thereby making the best use of your time.

Possible outcomes from using this book

Depending on which parts of the book you work through, by the end of your reading and work you should:

Know:

- some strategies for ensuring that your study time is used effectively
- how to look after your key resources of motivation, energy and concentration
- some things to do when you are 'stuck'
- how to gain access to other resources both on- and offline.

Understand:

- how to make the best use of different modes of study
- that learning mathematics effectively involves both 'doing'

mathematics and reflecting on that doing, requiring both being engaged in mathematical activity and standing back from that work in order to think and reflect.

Be aware of the dangers of:

- simply filling in time rather than studying constructively
- telling yourself that you understand when you do not.

Task 1.3 Reading

What are you going to do next?

Do you actually need to work through the next chapter? How can you find out without first having to do it?

Comment

A good way to find out is to skim through the chapter, paying particular attention to the various headings (but not reading anything in detail). Perhaps make marks against sections you want to:

- work on in detail
- read through quickly, to check whether you are familiar with the contents
- come back to at a later date
- ignore for now.

You could use the same process for the rest of the book.

2

Getting ready

This chapter is about the preparation (mental, physical and social) that you may need to do *before* starting a course of study. It is primarily designed for people who are relatively inexperienced at organising their own studies or have not studied for a while. Getting ready to start a course of study involves thinking about why you are going to study, how to find and manage study time, the people who will be involved, and the resources that will be needed.

FIRST STEPS

At school, there is often little choice about how, when and where studying is done, but for university study there is a great deal of flexibility – and greater temptation to do other things. Because there is less guidance and imposed discipline, it is essential to adopt appropriate and efficient ways of studying. There are many strategies for improving the efficiency and effectiveness of study – you may already be aware of some of these, but there may be others you haven't thought of.

This book covers such issues as:

- being an active learner, rather than passively trying to absorb information and develop skill
- using and managing resources effectively for the way you best work, e.g. time, study materials, people
- understanding how the various components of a course can best be drawn on
- developing note-making processes that enhance your learning
- strategies for developing understanding, e.g. developing a greater fluency with 'speaking' mathematically, with drawing diagrams and making and using other forms of representation, with using Information and Communication Technology (ICT) to help you learn mathematics
- different approaches to solving problems

- ways of increasing your marks in coursework assignments and examinations.

What is studying about?

It is not sufficient to read through the course materials and even to carry out the tasks suggested. To appreciate, understand, remember and be able to apply the knowledge and processes described and discussed in them requires much more active involvement on your part. Studying can be considered to have three stages, all of which are interrelated and contribute to the whole process:

- prior preparation, including getting an overview, scheduling time, working on preparatory materials
- learning through attending lectures and tutorials, reading and making notes, doing practice examples, and so on
- reviewing particular knowledge, processes and learning approaches.

While you are studying, you need to think about:

- what you are learning
- where you are having problems
- what makes things easier for you.

A good way of doing this is to make brief notes as you go along and keep them in a learning file or journal. These need not just be notes about course content, but could also include comments about:

- how, where and when you learn best
- good strategies for coping with challenging work
- what to do if you get stuck.

You will need to reflect on your learning throughout the course – this is an active and important part of effective study. It can be good for your morale to realise how much your knowledge, skill and understanding is developing.

Why study mathematics?

There are a number of reasons why people embark on a particular course of study. For example:

- to improve understanding of a subject or topic
- to gain a recognised qualification
- to improve employment opportunities
- as part of a wider programme of study
- to improve self-confidence
- to support someone else
- for general interest or as a leisure activity
- to fulfil an ambition.

Task 2.1 What are some of your reasons?

Think about the reasons for studying listed above – which ones are true for you and can you add any more? Now list your reasons for studying mathematics below, putting them in order, with the one(s) most important to you first.

My reasons for studying mathematics

| |
| |
| |
| |

Hint: use a pencil – your reasons may evolve over time.

What are some of your hopes and aspirations surrounding mathematics for the short and the longer term?

My aspirations

Short term	Longer term

What are your main concerns about studying mathematics? List them here.

My main concerns

| |
| |
| |
| |

Hint: put copies of your lists where you can see them.

Comment

Knowing your main aims will help you to plan your studies, while keeping them in mind will help your motivation should the going get tough. If you have concerns, then these need to be addressed – and this book is designed to help you plan how to do so effectively.

Concerns about studying mathematics often stem from previous experiences.

Task 2.2 Thinking back

Think about your previous experiences of learning mathematics. Which aspects did you enjoy and what did you find least interesting or most problematic?

Comment
Mathematics is one of those subjects that people tend to love or hate.

If you have had problems in the past, you are not alone (most of the adult population in the UK feel as you do). This can be for a variety of reasons, but often stems from unfortunate experiences at school: for example, teaching approaches that did not suit your learning style or not knowing how to work on your understanding. Now, by using this book (particularly Chapter 6), you have the opportunity to learn in ways that may suit you better.

On the other hand, if you have always enjoyed mathematics and not had too many problems, you may still find that you need to make adjustments to meet the demands of learning mathematics at degree level.

There are three main differences between school and university mathematics.

1 *The pace of delivery and level of support.* At school, the teacher may have explained material several times until most of the class understood, with extra support for those who were struggling. At university, material will be presented once and it is up to you to 'get it'. This means many more concepts and results are presented per session, so it can be easy to lose the thread. It is up to you to work through your notes and be familiar with the concepts before the next session. There may be some tutorial support, though at nowhere near the level available at school. At school, there tend to be exercises on each topic so you get plenty of practice, whereas at university there may only be one or two examples per topic – if you find you need extra practice, you may have to find more examples for yourself in textbooks, problem collections or old examination papers.

2 *The level of abstraction.* University mathematics is largely concerned with the study of different types of mathematical objects (such as functions, matrices, groups) and general properties and results

(theorems) about them, rather than solely specific examples or computational techniques. Calculations tend to involve symbols and variables with unspecified values (parameters) rather than numbers. This is particularly true for topics in pure mathematics and provides a substantial step-difference from the level of generality and abstraction met in most school mathematics. While some topics are obviously 'pure' (concerned with solving problems within mathematics itself) and others 'applied' (concerned with solving problems outside mathematics), the boundaries are less clear-cut and there tends to be more overlap than in school topics.

3 *The degree of rigour*. A lot of university mathematics is concerned with proving statements are true and precisely specifying under what conditions they are valid. For example, if a solution only relates to the counting numbers then this has to be stated as 'for all positive integers'. Any assumptions made need to be specified in precise terms: for example, 'assuming the angle θ lies in the range $0 < \theta < 2\pi$', i.e. less than one complete rotation.

Keys to effective study

There are a number of 'keys' to effective and successful study, including:

- being and staying motivated
- being organised
- being physically and mentally fit for study
- having support when necessary.

Getting organised involves making the most of time, energy, people and resources.

FINDING AND MANAGING TIME

When you start studying, whether full- or part-time, the shape of your life changes. Effective study often requires quite a lot of time, and time in fairly good-sized chunks at that, not just for learning and doing mathematics, but also for thinking about and mulling over ideas. You will have to make space in your life.

Students regularly have to make difficult choices between competing calls on their time. It is likely that the time required for study will displace some other activity, so you have to become an expert at creating time – or at least an efficient user of it. One way to set about this is to draw up a chart of your typical week and see where there is room for manoeuvre.

Initially, for full-time students, it can seem like there is plenty of time in a week, because there are relatively few fixed events such as lectures or tutorials. However, the guideline is that full-time studying should take up a 'normal' working week of around 40 hours. Without a disciplined approach to time management, self-study time evaporates and catching up can prove difficult.

Part-time and distance-learning students usually have less flexibility, with more demands on their time and energy. It is worth trying different patterns of study, in order to find the one most suitable to your life, personality and learning style for the particular subject being studied.

Task 2.3 Plan for this week

Complete the chart below or draw up your own version, perhaps including more divisions than just morning, afternoon and evening. (If you have access to a computer, you might do this using a spreadsheet program or a calendar application.)

Mark in regular activities and the time you can reasonably expect to be able to set aside for studying this book and mark where in the week it falls. Try to identify where clashes are likely to occur (friends expecting you to go out, that important sports fixture, etc.) and where you may have to rearrange or even cut back on some things in order to create study time.

Timetable

	Sunday	Monday	Tuesday	Wednesday	Thursday	Friday	Saturday
Morning							
Afternoon							
Evening							

Comment

Do not be alarmed if you found this task almost impossible. It is. Life is usually extremely messy. What's more, having made a plan, it is even harder to stick to it. But sticking to it is not necessarily the point. Even if you find that you are constantly having to amend your plan, it is still worth making the effort, because the decisions you make in changing plans force you to think about what you are doing and why. Planning helps you to think strategically rather than just drifting. It puts you in charge. Knowing that a planned study period has been lost makes you aware that you need to make up that missed time.

At the end of the week, review how you have performed against your plan. Write in what actually happened – when and for what did you get diverted or distracted? Then make a new plan for next week. It would be worth keeping and comparing your amended weekly plans over a period of time to see if any pattern emerges. This will help you to understand the problems of being in charge of your own study.

When you start your course, make sure you create your own plan for each week. Some courses provide longer-term study planners; if yours does not, draw up your own longer-term plans so that you can keep a check on approaching deadlines, family occasions or other events that will have an effect on your available study time.

Using each study session effectively

You need to be aware of what needs to be done and then to prioritise your tasks. One method is to classify tasks according to their urgency and importance, as shown in Table 2.1.

Table 2.1 Priorities

	IMPORTANT	UNIMPORTANT
URGENT	1. Important and urgent, e.g. consolidation work on today's lecture notes to ensure they will be understandable tomorrow	2. Unimportant but urgent, e.g. low-scoring assignment due in a couple of days
NOT URGENT	3. Important but not urgent, e.g. work on understanding of new concept before next week	4. Unimportant and not urgent, e.g. rewrite notes in best handwriting

The point is not to sacrifice priority 2 items for priority 3 ones. While keeping relative priorities in mind is essential, you also need to be aware of those tasks that need total alertness and those that can be tackled when tired or somewhat distracted.

When you have decided which task to work on, then you need to give it your full concentration. Work at it single-mindedly as long as it seems productive to some extent. Frequently, when working on a mathematical task, you may need to 'struggle on, vaguely hoping for the best'. Once you reach the stage where work is no longer productive (though also see the comments at the end of Chapter 6 on what to do when you are stuck) – or the task is finished – move on to something else.

Beware of time-filling on relatively trivial tasks (priority 4 ones) at the expense of more important work: for example, passively reading the whole of this book rather than actively working on the specific sections you need most! You need to work efficiently to be effective and to be efficient you need to manage the tasks to be done.

It is worth thinking about prioritising the non-study aspects of your life too.

- Expect to study for 40 hours a week (or for the part-time equivalent number of hours).

- Set aside sizeable 'chunks' of time for concentrating on important tasks.

- Prioritise study tasks.

- Be prepared to struggle, but know what to do when stuck.

- Beware of time-filling.

GETTING THE RIGHT RESOURCES ORGANISED

Organise the right resources before the start of your course, so that the early weeks of study can be fully productive. Forethought can also save you unnecessary expense.

Study setting

To study efficiently and effectively, you need to be alert and to concentrate for varying but substantial amounts of time. The different modes of study are covered in more detail in the next chapter, but a lot of your time will be spent working on course materials on your own. You need to think about what would be ideal surroundings for you and then ensure that you organise things to be as close to that ideal as you can. This may entail having different spaces available at different times or for different activities, particularly if you are working at home.

Ideally, you need somewhere that is:

- quiet with no distractions
- comfortable (but not too comfortable), with adequate heating and good lighting
- organised and equipped for study.

Having a particular place set aside for your studies, with course materials to hand and study schedules visible, helps to establish a study ethos. If you are living with other people, you may have to negotiate particular times or signals (e.g. student room door closed) for when your chosen area is sacrosanct and off-limits.

For some people, silence when studying mathematics is imperative; for others, background music can help shut out other erratic aural distractions. Some people need space to move about, while others can only work best without visible clutter. Whatever works best for you is worth trying to achieve – what is best may vary for different types of activity, so be prepared to try different study environments if you find that your attention is wandering.

For some students living at home, the problems of finding a suitable study area can seem insurmountable. If this is your situation, then you need to think creatively. The following are some of the many strategies that have been used by students:

- Store study materials in boxes, crates or bags so they can be used in different places at different times.
- Ask your employer if your place of work can be used before or after work.
- Study in the kitchen late at night or very early in the morning.
- Work in the local library or at a friendly neighbour's house.
- Become a babysitter or sleeper-in for an elderly person.
- Get a partner, friend or relative to take the children out.
- Get earphones for the family television (or for yourself).

Equipment

There is a variety of useful equipment for working on mathematics, as you will soon discover when you want it to be at hand and it is not.

Pen and paper
Mathematics is essentially a practical discipline in that it is learned by doing rather than solely by reading about it. Although in some senses the 'doing' is mostly a mental activity, the stages of getting to a solution or proof need to be captured, so pen and paper tend to be essential items for studying mathematics. You will need to build up your own stationery store of such things as paper (plain or lined, hole-punched is ideal), graph paper, pen(s), pencil(s), highlighters for annotating text and notes, index tags or Post-it notes.

Calculator
For many mathematics courses (though not all), a calculator is necessary. For some, a particular model is specified; for others, there are limitations on the type of calculator that can be used in examinations. So check your university course details before buying one.

Calculators are not only for simply doing mathematics, they can also be powerful learning tools. There are sophisticated large-screen models available capable of algebraic manipulation, geometric construction and statistical functions. It may be that you end up with two calculators, one for use in examinations and a more powerful one to aid your learning and understanding.

For more on using computers and calculators, see Chapters 7 and 8.

Computer access
For some mathematics courses, access to a computer is essential, but for others it is only desirable. For certain courses, there is a minimum

machine specification, so again do not rush out to buy one before checking. While owning your own machine may be ideal, there are many other ways of gaining computer access:

- university IT centres
- loan schemes
- through work (some employers are prepared to support part-time students)
- Internet cafés or public libraries.

Audio-visual resources

For some university courses, for example Open University courses, you may need access to video or audio playback facilities (cassette or CD), both for preparation and taking the course itself. Ideally, this equipment should be available where you plan to study.

Storage

In all likelihood, there will be several types of materials that you will need to keep and refer back to with varying degrees of frequency:

- general course and university information
- work plans and timetables
- mathematical work from units
- learning notes
- work towards assignments.

Whether you keep course-related work in one file or several separate ones is up to you – the point is to organise your work in a way that is going to be useful:

- during the course
- when revising for the examination
- after the course, perhaps in preparation for future courses or for work.

Any notes need some kind of reference to what you were doing (and perhaps when) if they are to make any sense when you look back in a few weeks' time.

The following may be useful for organising your work:

- ring binder(s) and dividers
- magazine boxes or home-made equivalents, for storing course materials
- hole punch and/or punched plastic pockets
- bookshelves, crates or bag (especially if your designated work space is used for other purposes at different times)
- cardboard or plastic folders for storing/transporting loose pages.

Other resources

Some distance-learning courses provide all the materials considered necessary for successful study, including preparatory material for getting your mathematics up to speed. But it can be helpful to have access to additional materials even for these courses. Part of your preparation for a course is finding and using these resources, both at home and your university site.

Books

Most universities provide lists of set books and recommended reading. It is worth trying to borrow copies from a library before committing yourself to purchase. How is the library organised? Are all the mathematics books together or are they in several different places according to context or type of application? Acquiring one or two books for preparatory work before the course starts is worthwhile – but find out whether the student union organises second-hand book sales during 'freshers' week. Most campuses have a bookshop and the big bookselling chains have online ordering services. (Using textbooks effectively is discussed in Chapters 3 and 5.)

Online resources

Students of The Open University have access to course-related electronic library resources and electronic conferences through their own personal web pages. Similar facilities operate in some other universities.

For all students, there is a wealth of material freely available through the Internet, both on study skills (many university mathematics departments have online student handbooks) and on different topics in mathematics. It is also possible to download certain software or find relevant mathematics applets with which to engage online.

Task 2.4 Things to get ready

Make a list of things you think you will need to get ready and do before the start of your course.

Comment

For example, check on your course's use of calculators and computers, buy stationery, prepare a study area, explore libraries and bookshops. But perhaps the most important thing to do is to work on some actual mathematics. (See Chapters 5 and 6 for ways of working on your mathematics.)

LOOKING AFTER PEOPLE

Although undertaking a course of study seems to be purely an individual matter, it in fact involves a large number of people to a varying extent. You will have responsibilities towards yourself, family, friends, fellow students, teaching staff and, perhaps, work colleagues. These may well be duties of care as well as a responsibility to do as well as possible on your chosen course. These same people can also provide personal, domestic and academic support, but will need your help to ensure their support is appropriate and timely.

Yourself

You need to be as fit as possible, both physically and mentally, to make the most of study time. Your key learning resources are motivation, energy and concentration. This means looking after yourself, so be sure to:

- Eat regularly and well (but not too well – overeating makes the brain sluggish).
- Remember alcohol is a depressant and consumption impairs thinking, so minimise consumption during periods when intensive mathematical thought is needed.
- Avoid getting overtired (it hinders concentration and makes you more vulnerable to infections).
- Take regular exercise (it gets the blood rushing round and so more oxygen goes to the brain) as it can relieve stress.
- Know how to deal with feelings of anxiety and stress when they arise: for example, take a brisk walk, have a quick swim, talk out worries with a friend (some find that yoga, or T'ai Chi can increase energy and decrease stress).
- Budget carefully to ensure that money worries do not impinge at critical times in your course. If you are a full-time student, but need to take paid employment, ensure that working hours are sufficiently flexible to avoid missing key elements of your course.
- Allocate appropriate time for friends, and domestic and leisure activities.

Try to plan your studies for when your energy level is high – if you are an 'owl', study at night; if a 'lark', then study in the early morning. If you have a low-energy spell, then consider dealing with domestic chores rather than studying – after all shopping, washing and cleaning still have to be done some time – but beware if you are using these regularly as reasons not to study.

Task 2.5 What works for you

List some things that increase your energy and motivation, and those that sap effort and concentration.

Motivators and Sappers

Motivators	Sappers

- Develop activities that increase your energy levels and motivate you to study.
- Reduce distractions and energy sappers.

Family, friends, colleagues and teaching staff

The other people in your life can help or hinder your studies – and often do both! Simply ignoring them will not solve anything, but there are things you can do to minimise the distractions and maximise the benefits.

Let people know what you are doing
Just telling people that you are undertaking a course of study and will not be able to give as much time or energy to them is a good start. Most people will respect your decision, but you may need to remind them occasionally – it is unreasonable to expect them to be as aware of this as you need to be. Perhaps suggest times that you can be available and times when you would appreciate no interruptions or distractions.

Involve people in your studies
Talking to other people about your studies can greatly help on several levels:

- Close friends and family feel included rather than excluded from your new studying life (particularly relevant for parents of young children).
- You can rehearse what you have learned, which helps memorisation.

- You hear yourself talking confidently about some aspects, but perhaps being more hesitant about others, which can help focus future study.
- The people you are talking to may raise issues you had not considered.

Develop study partners
Try to find at least one person who is doing the same or a similar course with whom you can discuss new ideas and possible problems, or perhaps join a self-help group (see Chapter 3).

Get to know the teaching staff
Although the level of support from teachers is different at university from at school, academic support is still available. However, you may need to be more active in seeking it out. You will need to find out who are the staff attached to your course (lecturers and tutors) and how to contact them. In conventional universities, this may be by phone, by e-mail or by leaving notes on the doors of their offices.

Distance-learning students have an assigned tutor and particular ways of contacting her or him. For example, every student of The Open University has a tutor for each course they take, who is responsible for providing locally-based face-to-face tutorials, marking and commenting on assignments and providing personal telephone and/or e-mail assistance when requested. In addition, there are often central academics available for consultation about each course.

- Building up a relationship with your tutor can be crucial to effective study.

REFLECTION

'The best can be the enemy of the good': there comes a point when to say 'that is good enough' and go on to other things is a better use of time than to continue to work on a task that is already well enough completed. There are also times when you are struggling or are stuck when it is better to stop and go on to something else. (See Chapter 6 for more on strategies for what to do if you get stuck mathematically.) So, as well as being disciplined, you also need to be flexible and occasionally take stock of how you are working, as well as what you have done and have yet to do.

Task 2.6 So far, so ...

What have you achieved so far?

Have you been actively working with this text or being fairly passive in the face of it?

Have you completed the checklists, made some study plans, found a good place and time to work?

Are you ready to start thinking about ways of studying mathematics?

Have you got a study plan for working on other parts of this book (see Task 2.3)?

What are you going to do now before moving on to the next chapter you want to work on – how can you best use the time available?

Comment

Perhaps draw up your plans for the next couple of weeks or use the outline below.

A two-week timetable

	Sunday	Monday	Tuesday	Wednesday	Thursday	Friday	Saturday
Morning							
Afternoon							
Evening							
	Sunday	Monday	Tuesday	Wednesday	Thursday	Friday	Saturday
Morning							
Afternoon							
Evening							

- Have a clear aim for your studies.
- Manage study time effectively.
- Organise study space, equipment and resources.
- Look after yourself and others.
- Seek out people who can help you.
- Think about what you are learning and how you study most effectively.

3

Ways of studying

To make the most of your mathematical ability and powers, you need to be committed to studying effectively. Learning mathematics at a higher level is much more than acquiring and remembering facts and techniques. It involves making sense of new ideas for yourself and learning how to use them in different contexts. This chapter introduces various modes of study activity, together with suggestions about ways of making them more effective for you. Some of these are developed further in later chapters. (Remember to skim through the sub-headings and make a plan for studying this chapter before reading in detail.)

THE DIVERSITY OF STUDY

During your course, information will be made available to you in a variety of ways. For students following a traditional course of study, most information comes from:

- lectures
- lecture notes
- tutorials.

For distance-learning students, some or all of these are replaced by:

- written material (course units)
- audio and video cassettes, CDs or TV programmes
- tutorials (face-to-face, telephone or electronic)
- telephone, e-mail or computer-conferencing contact.

For all mathematics students, these may be supplemented by:

- recommended textbooks
- mathematical computer software
- conversations with other students.

Equally important is the work that you do on your own. Some work will be just for yourself and will not be seen by other people:

- making notes
- doing practice examples
- problem-solving
- working on understanding
- investigation and research
- learning and revising.

Other work is to be seen and possibly evaluated by others:

- doing assignments
- writing up project work
- preparing and giving presentations
- discussion and explanation, both informally and in tutorials
- answering examination questions.

Using different modes of study

Using a variety of modes of study can make a valuable contribution to your learning. It allows you to switch between different kinds of activity, to keep your mind alert, to make studying more interesting or sometimes to find a new way forward when you find yourself 'stuck'.

Learning involves the brain processing information received from the senses in such a way that it can be recalled and applied when needed. New information and ideas add to or amend ideas and information already known. Different parts of the brain process varied kinds or forms of information. In practice, this means that different types of activities involve various parts of the brain and associations can be built up which then make recall easier. This is why making notes of things you have heard or seen, talking to other people, drawing diagrams or using mathematical software packages can all help to make your learning more successful.

Learning mathematics involves gaining familiarity with concepts, results and theorems and developing a facility with methods and techniques (whether computational or connected with proof), but to be able to use mathematics successfully in varying contexts implies a much greater understanding. There are different ways of gaining this deeper understanding. In some circumstances, it is best to work on understanding the big idea first and then apply this understanding to particular examples – a move from *generalising* to *specialising*. Sometimes it is necessary to work on concepts and techniques, by doing a large number of examples and then going to work on getting an overview – a move from *specialising* to *generalising*. Perhaps the most successful approach is to keep both these main lines of approach in mind, while using a variety of ways of working. (See Chapter 6 for more on specialising and generalising and different ways of working mathematically.)

Study skills

Gaining and improving study skills is a process geared towards becoming an effective, independent learner. Remember, this process includes:

- making and sustaining good practical arrangements
- looking after yourself physically and mentally, including keeping your spirits up
- systematically analysing and prioritising study activity, both in the short and the longer term
- developing a range of ways of working
- finding out and using the resources available to support your learning
- regularly reviewing what works for you.

- To make the most of your mathematical abilities, it is worth making the effort to develop effective study habits.

- There are many ways of studying, each of which helps your learning in different ways. This variety makes studying more interesting and helps you to learn in depth.

- Learn to use different approaches on the same task in order to maximise associations and connections.

The rest of this chapter is about:

- studying on your own
- learning with other people
- making and keeping notes
- learning through reading.

STUDYING ON YOUR OWN

Higher education courses expect you to be responsible for organising your own study. If you are following a conventional university course, the given lecture and tutorial timetable will be the basis of your study plan. Establish early on in the term or semester how many assignments you are expected to complete and when they are due. Expect to work 40 hours per week (pro rata for part-time study), including the timetabled hours, allowing time for:

- working on your notes between lectures
- working on assignments and projects
- recommended reading
- using the library.

Try to find a good place to work at the university in the gaps between lectures, when you may not have time to go back to your accommodation. This may be the library, a designated student workroom or a teaching room that is not in use. Ask your tutor for advice if it is not obvious where you can work.

Distance-learning students will normally receive a timetable indicating which course units are to be studied in which weeks and giving the dates when assignments are due. Ideally, try to work a little ahead of this schedule to allow for unexpected events that can unavoidably disrupt your study plans. You will be given guidance on how many hours you should expect to work on your studies each week.

Whatever course you are following, you need to allow yourself sufficient long and uninterrupted study periods each week (several hours at a time); use these for mathematical thinking and to immerse yourself in your work. Shorter tasks and those requiring less concentration can be done in odd moments between other activities.

It is a good idea to keep a list of 'things to do' (together with completion dates) and to be aware of which tasks are going to need most time and concentration. In studying mathematics, you will continually be moving into territory that is new to you, so it can be very difficult to know how long a given task is going to take. You may easily solve a problem in about half an hour or you may struggle with it for two days, before perhaps deciding you need to ask for help. You need to develop your own strategies to enable you to keep track of where you are gaining or losing time. A detailed study timetable can assist some people, but may not be the best use of your time – you need to decide what is best for you. It may help to keep a running list of questions and problems, so that you can make the most of any opportunities that arise to discuss them with other students, a lecturer or tutor, or to look things up in the library.

LEARNING WITH OTHER PEOPLE

Much learning is, in some sense, a collective activity – you learn by engaging with other people's thoughts, whether through the medium of lectures, tutorials, textbooks or informal discussions.

At school, these phases of study tend to be controlled by the teacher, while the student has relatively little control. At university level, *you* are responsible for managing your own learning to a much greater extent. Success depends, in part, on making the change from more passive to more active learning early on in your university studies.

Lectures

Lectures are the formal teaching element of a traditional university course. (For distance-learning students, the content of lectures is presented in written course units – see the following section.) A mathematics lecture normally lasts about an hour and, at the beginning of your course, you may have up to 12 in a week. The form of a lecture varies enormously from university to university and from lecturer to lecturer, but you are likely to be in a large group of students, not all of whom will be following the same course as you.

At their best, lectures are lively, interactive, thought-provoking and highly motivating; at their worst, they can be boring, difficult to follow and sleep-inducing. Their purpose is to present and explain new ideas, concepts, techniques and processes, and demonstrate ways of working on mathematics. Ideally, lecturers use a range of visual aids (including mathematical software), verbalise their thinking processes, encourage the asking of questions and possibly provide outline lecture notes.

Regardless of the quality of the lectures, aim for 100% attendance. Regardless of almost anything, make sure you obtain a good, complete set of notes (see the next section on making and keeping notes).

Practicalities
You will make the most of your lecture course if you are well prepared in a practical way:

- Get enough sleep the night before and avoid excessive intake of alcohol.
- Make sure you have an accurate record of the times and places of all your lectures.
- Take everything you need with you – writing materials, paper, notebook, lecture notes.
- Arrive on time or a little early – use any spare time to look through your notes from the previous lecture.
- Try to sit in a well-lit, well-ventilated spot, in the front third of the lecture room.

It is important to realise that you are not going to be able to understand a course of lectures unless you do some work between lectures. Imagine, for example, you are attending a lecture course on a topic called 'Metric Spaces'. In the first lecture, the definition of a metric space is given. In lecture 8, you are given the definition of a compact metric space (which depends on some of the concepts introduced in lectures 1 to 7). Just before the end of lecture 9, the concept of the Bolzano–Weierstrass property is introduced. Then, in lecture 10, it is proved that a metric space is compact if and only if it has the Bolzano–Weierstrass property. What chance do you have of understanding lecture 10 if you have not understood and remembered the concepts 'compact' from lecture 8 and 'Bolzano–Weierstrass property' from lecture 9?

- Expect mathematics lectures to take you into uncharted territory.
- Unless you familiarise yourself with the ground covered so far, you are not going to understand the next steps.

On a practical level, there are several possible strategies:

- Turn yourself into a non-thinking note-taker, just writing everything down and hoping you can make sense of it later.
- Attempt to understand as much as possible during lectures – work on understanding your notes between lectures and try to familiarise yourself with the concepts of each lecture before the next one.

Being a non-thinking note-taker is both boring and tiring, but there may be times when you have to do it anyway. No matter how well prepared you are, it can always happen in the course of an hour's lecture that you reach a point where you can no longer follow, let alone understand, what the lecturer is saying.

Being well prepared and understanding as much as possible is the ideal – do it for as much of the time as you can.

During a lecture
Be an active participant by:

- being responsive (e.g. nod when you have followed something, look puzzled when you have not, try to signal if the pace is too fast for you – you are unlikely to be the only one)
- making your own clear, well-spaced notes, especially on anything the lecturer does on a board or overhead projector slide
- avoiding causing irrelevant distractions to the lecturer or fellow students
- asking questions – if your lecturer does not take questions during the lecture, make a note of things you need to ask at the end. Asking questions during a lecture can take courage to do, but other students will be grateful and it is not helpful to yourself to pretend you understand when you do not.

Tutorials
Tutorials, supervisions, seminars and workshops are all forms of group study. They may last from 20 minutes (for example, an individual telephone tutorial for a distance-learning student) to two hours and can

involve from 1 to 20 students working with a tutor. The session may be
for introducing a new topic, joint working on examples, presentation of
work, revision or 'troubleshooting'.

The important aspect of a tutorial is that it provides an opportunity
for direct interaction between the tutor's expertise and your understanding. For maximum benefit, you need to be actively engaged, which
implies being prepared beforehand and ready to take part in discussions
and when examples are being worked through.

To make the most of tutorials, it is useful to consider the three phases:

- preparation
- activity
- reflection.

Preparation is crucial to understanding and being able to contribute. If
you know that certain problems or exercises are to be discussed, have a
reasonable attempt at them before the tutorial. This way, even if you
cannot solve them completely, you will be familiar with the material and
have any relevant definitions, theorems and other results at your fin-
gertips.

Have a list of specific questions you want to ask your tutor – points
arising from the lectures, difficulties with problems or exercises, or wider
questions you might have. If you have fallen behind with your studies,
you can ask for help on how best to catch up.

During the tutorial, play as active a part as you can by:

- responding to any questions asked by the tutor
- volunteering to share your solutions to exercises and problems
- seeking clarification if you do not understand
- asking for an explanation to be repeated
- requesting additional examples
- asking your prepared questions.

This too can take some courage – try to overcome the fear of making a
fool of yourself. Even the most elementary question deserves a considered response from the tutor and there will often be other students in
the group with similar difficulties.

If an atmosphere of participation and cooperation can be fostered in
your tutorial groups (this depends on both the students and the tutor),
you will find them a lot more interesting and memorable. However, do
not indulge in self-recrimination if you are too shy to ask your questions
in front of the others; simply ask the tutor at the end of the session.

After the tutorial, ask yourself if you have made the most of it:

- Did you obtain the information you needed?
- How fully did you participate?
- Is there anything you would do differently next time?

Self-help groups

Try to find people who are doing the same or a similar course with whom you can discuss new ideas and possible problems – self-help groups can enhance your studies and provide support. They can be particularly valuable when revising for examinations. Such groups can meet face-to-face, talk over the telephone or communicate via e-mail or electronic conferencing. (These activities need to be focused on specific study topics, otherwise they can become unproductive time-wasters.)

Active and constructive cooperation between fellow students can greatly enhance understanding and work quality. Helping a fellow student can be highly productive for both parties.

> Working with tutors and fellow students:
>
> • can help you to get a sense of new ideas and how they connect with your existing knowledge
>
> • helps you to become more fluent in speaking and writing mathematical language
>
> • can be a source of practical help
>
> • encourages you to maintain study schedules
>
> • can help boost confidence, by sharing study worries with other people.

MAKING AND KEEPING NOTES

Whichever study activity you undertake, you will need to make notes of some description. Some, such as lecture notes, will serve as a more or less permanent record of what you have studied. Other notes, such as specific question notes, are more temporary and may be discarded once they have fulfilled their purpose.

Note-making is a way of processing information. It can involve:

• selecting content that is relevant (and discarding or ignoring that which is irrelevant)
• condensing some elements to emphasise and stress the essence
• expanding some elements to clarify meaning.

Lecture notes

Usually, note-taking in mathematics lectures is straightforward because, if you are intended to take notes, the lecturer will usually write everything down in a precise way. This is not the case for all subjects, but exactness and attention to detail are essential in mathematics. Some lecturers will provide duplicated lecture notes. These may cover all the material of the lectures (or even more) or they may simply be skeleton notes, outlining the main points.

Even if complete printed notes are provided, many students still prefer to make their own notes in addition. There is something about writing mathematics in your own handwriting that makes it more familiar and more accessible. On the other hand, it can be difficult to write notes and listen attentively at the same time, so if complete notes are provided beforehand you may decide just to annotate and highlight these in lectures, rather than taking your own notes. The main thing is to obtain and personalise a complete set of notes. In addition, it is often helpful to note down informal explanations, diagrams or examples that shed light on the more formal material.

Write up your notes between lectures
This has several advantages:

- You can write more legibly as you will not be hurried.
- You can amalgamate notes taken in lectures with any duplicated notes and perhaps add notes from textbooks.
- It is a useful way of familiarising yourself with the material.
- It helps you notice if there is anything you do not understand.
- It is a valuable way of preparing for the next lecture on the subject.

Of course, it is essential to store your lecture notes safely and in the right order. It is well worth checking that each set of notes has a title, page numbers and a date, just in case they get muddled.

Notes from study modules

Distance-learning students have a similar choice to make about taking notes. Do you make complete notes of your own or do you simply annotate and highlight the written text material provided?

The positive points for making your own notes are:

- It helps you familiarise yourself with the material (see the later section in this chapter on learning through reading).
- Written study materials necessarily contain complete explanations of absolutely everything, so they can be somewhat long-winded – your own notes can be more concise and geared to your own degree of understanding.
- Note-taking enables you to combine material from different sources – written, audio, video and computer resources can be amalgamated into a single document.
- The notes can form a useful basis for your revision later on.

The disadvantage of making your own formal notes is the length of time it can take. Distance-learning materials are usually of high quality, so you might decide against taking notes, instead simply annotating, highlighting and perhaps tagging pages where the most important results are given. Alternatively, as part of the learning process, you might find it helpful to make very brief notes of new ideas, symbols, etc. to develop your own glossary, perhaps using a card index.

Notes from textbooks

If you look something up in a textbook or spend time studying a longer section, it makes sense to note down the essential details for future reference (again, see the later section on learning through reading). As well as avoiding the need to look up the same information twice, it will also help to fix it in your mind. You could either keep a separate notebook for these notes or introduce the information into your lecture or study notes at appropriate points. The notes should include a reference to the particular book and page, in case you need to refer back at any stage.

Task 3.1 Making notes

Think about how you might make notes from a textbook – use the following extract as an example.

In this section we shall develop an arithmetic of numbers such as $5 + \sqrt{-15}$, involving the square roots of negative numbers. We begin by introducing some notation. For any positive real number r, we can write:

$$\sqrt{-r} = \sqrt{r(-1)} = \sqrt{r}\sqrt{-1}$$

where $\sqrt{r}$ is taken to mean the positive square root. Since $r > 0$, $\sqrt{r}$ is just a real number, so we can express the square roots of all negative numbers as a real multiple of the square root of -1. Leonhard Euler (1707–83) introduced the symbol i for $\sqrt{-1}$, and using this we have $\sqrt{-r} = (\sqrt{r}).i$ which can be written more succinctly as $\sqrt{r}\,i$.

Using this notation, we can, for example, write $5 + \sqrt{-15}$ as $5 + \sqrt{15}i$. So, using i, we can represent all the new numbers with which we shall be concerned.

Complex numbers
- A **complex number** is of the form $a + bi$, where a and b may be any real numbers and where $i^2 = -1$.
- We use $\mathbb{C}$ to represent the set of all complex numbers.

- For a complex number $z = a + bi$, we call a the **real part** of z and b the **imaginary part** of z. We write Re(z) for the real part, a, and Im(z) for the imaginary part, b.

Notice that the 'imaginary part' of a complex number is a real number. So, for example, the imaginary part of the complex number $3 - 5i$ is -5 (*not* $-5i$).

Examples of complex numbers are $3 + 4i$, $12 - 5i$ and $-1 - 2i$. However, there is no restriction on the real numbers that can be used as the real and the imaginary parts. They can be rationals like $\frac{3}{2}$, roots like $\sqrt{2}$, numbers like π or any combination of such real numbers.

In particular, $0 + 2i$, $-3 + 0i$ and $0 + 0i$ are all complex numbers, and for simplicity we write these numbers as $2i$, -3 and 0 respectively, omitting 0s where possible. Also, we usually write numbers like $3 + 1i$ and $-1 - 1i$ as $3 + i$ and $-1 - i$ respectively, suppressing the redundant symbol 1.

Open University Course Exploring Mathematics MS221
Chapter D1 p. 11

Comment

Your reaction to this task is likely to be dependent on your level of mathematical knowledge. If you are familiar and confident with the notion of complex numbers, you may not have made any notes, or you may have highlighted a section you thought gave a particularly succinct definition. On the other hand, if this was a new topic, you might have written down something like:

A complex number is a number of the form $a + bi$, where a and b may be any real numbers and $\mathbb{C}$ is the set of complex numbers (just as $\mathbb{R}$ is used for set of real numbers, $\mathbb{N}$ for set of natural numbers, $\mathbb{Z}$ for the set of all integers and $\mathbb{Q}$ for set of quotients, i.e. rational numbers).

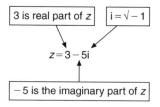

Figure 3.1 Example of complex number $z = 3 - 5i$, where $i^2 = -1$.

Notes from non-written sources

For sources such as audio cassettes, videotapes or work done with mathematical computer packages, you need to decide whether to take notes or not. It may be that you are best just watching, listening or working on the computer and learning from the experience, and then making notes on the points that are important to you at the end. Alternatively, you may want to stop from time to time to note down the important points.

Notes for assignments

Read through any assignment you are given well before the due date and make sure you understand the questions (if you do not, clarify matters with your tutor). Make a note of anything you come across that might be helpful (relevant definitions, theorems or examples from your lecture notes or study materials, information from discussion with other students, hints given by the lecturer or tutor, and so on), as well as any ideas that come to you for solving the problems. These are just temporary notes, so they do not need to be particularly tidy, just kept together until you have completed the assignment (see Chapter 4 for more on assignments).

Once the assignment is finished, read any feedback carefully and assess how it can help you with future assignments.

Revision notes

Many students make notes in a condensed form to help them learn for examinations. Different colours, highlights and diagrams can all help you remember. You may decide to discard these notes after the examination (see Chapter 4 for more on preparing for examinations).

Other types of notes

You may find it worth keeping some notes that are not related to specific course content: for example, mathematical or study-skill items that are likely to be of use throughout your degree studies.

A 'mathematical gems' notebook

You may find a mathematical gem of any kind – that is, something which speaks clearly to you:

- a clear definition or helpful explanation of a mathematical word or symbol
- an illuminating example
- an interesting theorem
- a clever proof
- a clear explanation of a tricky point
- an unusual way of remembering something.

In fact, for anything at all that appeals to you, it makes sense to make a note of it. First, for the sheer enjoyment of having your favourite pieces of mathematics to hand and, second, because you never know when it might come in useful. In the course of your years of study, you should be able to create quite a collection. It may be worth having separate sections: for instance, have one that is a personal mathematical dictionary.

Using a learning journal

A journal, or study diary, can be a useful confidence-building resource. The idea is to keep a notebook in which you record details of each 'critical incident' in your mathematical studies. For a few courses, keeping a learning journal is essential because there are assignments that ask you to reflect on your learning. A critical incident is any event in your studies that arouses strong emotion. For example:

- moments of illumination
- amazing flashes of intuition
- times when you feel confident and well prepared
- when you make a good presentation
- when you get good marks
- times when you succeed, times when you get hopelessly stuck
- times when you do not understand
- when you (perhaps embarrassingly) are unable to explain something
- times when you cannot do your assignments
- when your marks are disappointingly low
- times when you feel like giving it all up
- amusing incidents.

Write down the date of the incident, recording what happened briefly but vividly, and how you felt. Notice the choices you made in dealing with the situation and consider other alternatives you might have chosen. In particular, note any successful strategies for future reference.

A journal can help you in the following ways:

- It can help to write things down if you have difficulties.
- Reading back over your journal will give you a sense of progress: for example, one day you might write in despair, 'I'll never understand these differential equations' and three weeks later you realise that you do understand them.
- It will help you to put your highs and lows in perspective.

Task 3.2 Pause for thought

Recall two memorable incidents from your latest period of mathematical study, one difficult and one pleasurable. What, if anything, did you learn from them at the time? Are there any useful lessons for your university studies?

Comment
Why not start your journal now and use these recollections as your first entries?

LEARNING THROUGH READING

Reading is one of the most common ways of encountering mathematics. What you will be asked or required to read will vary from course to course, but everyone will need to be able to read written mathematical text at some stage in their course.

Course units

For distance-learning students, the course units are the main teaching element. They are the equivalent of lectures for conventional students. (Most are written but some elements may be presented in the form of TV programmes or videotapes.)

Before starting a unit
Remind yourself of actions that may help your study:

- Skim through the unit – this will give you an overview and a chance to meet some of the ideas, vocabulary and symbols involved.
- Read through any associated assessment (assignment questions).
- Prepare your study area: check equipment, etc. is to hand, prepare your notebook (unit title, date, pre-number pages, etc.).
- Try to prevent distractions occurring: for example, tell other people that you are about to start studying.
- Check through any previous related notes to ensure that you still understand – this is the equivalent of warming up for a sport activity and gets your brain ready.

While working on a unit
Be a more active learner by:

- Making your own clear, well-spaced notes, especially of any activities or tasks.

- Using various strategies to keep concentration and avoid time-filling: for example, play quiet music to mask distracting noises off, set intermediate targets with rewards, walk about occasionally, say things out loud.
- Making notes of things you need to ask your tutor either by phone or at your next tutorial – this can take courage to do the first few times, but if you do not ask for help when you need it, you may be left with an unwelcome and unhelpful gap in your knowledge.

At the end of a study session

When working through a course unit, it is all too easy to think you have understood when in fact you have just been able to follow: this is particularly true of well-written units, just as with well-prepared lectures. There are various strategies for checking on the robustness of your understanding.

- Work through your own notes, supplementing them and clarifying any symbols you have used. They might make sense immediately after doing the work – but will they in a week or two? Highlight the main new ideas.
- File everything, making sure it is all titled and dated.
- Re-read associated assignment questions to check whether these now seem straightforward.
- Make a list of the things you need to work on, such as further practice examples (including assignment questions). Annotate the list with the items you need to discuss further with your tutor or fellow students.
- Tell a friend about what you have been studying. Trying to put your learning into spoken words will help you to get an overview and let you hear where you are uncertain. (The friend does not have to be knowledgeable about the subject matter: in fact, it can often help more if they are not.) You may be pleasantly surprised about what you have learned. If there is no one around, then tell the dog, cat or goldfish!
- Think about how you prepared for the unit of work and what happened both during and after it. Did you make the most of the learning opportunity, or are there things you will do differently next time? For example, will you leave more space when making notes, or make better use of time by being clearer about what is essential? Do you need to take any actions to improve your morale or your physical well-being?
- Talk about the content to other students on your course – you may obtain additional insights – and putting your thoughts into words may both clarify your thinking and expose any gaps.

Textbooks

Every mathematical text is written with a specific readership in mind. Members of this readership have a particular level of mathematical preparation and are familiar with certain mathematical concepts, terms and symbols. How you react to a text will depend partly upon whether you have the necessary previous knowledge, i.e. how close you are to the author's 'model' reader. Your reaction could range from 'That's easy, I've done it before' to 'It's completely incomprehensible'. It is quite normal to come across material that falls into the latter category. If you cannot understand something, do not take it personally; very probably, you are not the only one (see Chapter 6 for some suggestions about what to do when you are 'stuck').

Most of what you read at the start of your studies will be from textbooks, lecture notes or other material prepared specifically for students. At the beginning of the text, a certain level of knowledge will be assumed (often this is outlined in the introduction, or you may be supplied with revision materials that explain this in more detail). In addition, it is likely that later chapters of the text will depend upon material in previous sections. Some texts give a flow diagram in the introduction showing how the various chapters interrelate.

Have pen and paper to hand
Understanding mathematics is an intensely personal experience – nobody can do it for you. In order to understand anything new, you have to become familiar with it and see how it fits in with what you already know. To do this, it is necessary to work with the material yourself and writing plays a major part in this – not formal notes, but rough notes, scribbles, trial diagrams and provisional calculations. Here are some suggestions.

- If the material seems easy, 'play' with it a little. For example, if a mathematical model uses an interest rate of 5%, what difference would it make if it were 10% or 50%? Or if a graph is shown of the equation $y = |x - 1|$, try to graph $y = |2x - 1|$ or $y = |x| - 1$.
- If there is a worked example in the text, try to do it yourself without looking at the book's solution (perhaps cover up the solution and reveal it line by line). Or look for another exercise you can do using the same method.
- Make a note of any new concepts or unfamiliar notation (add it to your personal dictionary). To understand something new, you must first be able to hold it in your mind and writing it down can help. For example, the text may say that $\log_b a = c$ means the same as $a = b^c$. Try writing it using different variable names (say, x, y, z instead of a, b, c) or by putting $b = 2$ or 10 to see what happens (a move referred to as *specialisation* in Chapter 6). You may decide that a

particular example, such as $\log_2 8 = 3$, is the best way of remembering the connection.

- Do the exercises (at least some of them). Think about what makes them examples of the particular topic or concept (the generality of them) – what is an easy example, what makes a difficult one (for more on this, see Chapter 6).
- There may be gaps for you in some mathematical arguments. Try to fill these in – for example, steps such as factoring, cancelling, multiplying out brackets then simplifying may be omitted in the text.
- Writing out a difficult passage can sometimes make it more accessible, because your brain is concentrating on each line. Try to write it out in your own words (more techniques for working on technical texts are provided in Chapter 5).
- If you are reading a theorem followed by its proof, write down the statement of the theorem to fix it in your mind *before* starting to work on understanding the proof. Ask yourself why the theorem is stated this way and whether all the conditions in it are necessary.
- Make sketches, draw diagrams – they do not have to be perfect to assist your brain in emphasising the important aspects.

Reading a longer section – selective reading
When you have a whole section to read your strategy will depend upon how 'light' or 'dense' the text is.

A relatively light text (no university-level mathematics text can really be classified as 'light reading') will probably be something like a user-friendly textbook or a self-study module. The important definitions and results may be displayed in boxes, there may be activities as well as exercises and problems, there will be a fair amount of informal explanation, there may be notes in the margin and possibly even cartoons and different colours.

A dense text will have a serious-sounding title such as *The Foundations of Modern Analysis*, no coloured ink or cartoons and only formal-looking 'diagrams', if any. The examples will contain significant amounts of mathematical notation, which will probably need unpacking. It will be written in a tightly logical fashion, so that you simply cannot dip into it unless you are already familiar with the material. You will have to read most, if not all, of the preceding material in order to understand a given section. Reading it will take much longer than just reading the words, as you may struggle for hours, days or even weeks to understand a small section. Any ideas of skimming it or planning to miss bits out are not useful, as you are unlikely to have sufficient knowledge to do this.

The terms 'light' and 'dense' are subjective and texts you now find very dense will seem to become more user-friendly as your mathematical knowledge increases. Of course, it is you rather than the text that has probably changed in the meantime.

If you are reading a reasonably light text, there are ways in which you can save time, as you may not need to read the section in order from beginning to end. Clearly you need to understand everything identified as important, either because it is in a box or because it is labelled 'Definition' or 'Theorem' or perhaps 'Method' or 'Summary'. You will usually need to read some of the preceding text to do this. Long-winded examples are prime candidates for passages to miss out (at least on initial reading). Typically, these will have titles such as 'For your further interest'. You may also find extended examples of particular techniques or calculations and feel that if you have grasped the main method these can be skipped over.

Dense texts do tend to have one advantage over light ones. They are usually very well organised, with a good index and consistent and systematic notation. All the definitions and theorems have numbers, which means they can be precisely referred to at other points in the text. Lighter texts are easier to read but not always so easy to navigate.

Task 3.3 Reading

Look at a few books on mathematics (possibly in a library or bookshop), including this one.

Give them each your personal 'density rating' from 0 to 20, 0 being totally light (e.g. *A Child's Guide to How Arithmetic Works*) to 20 being as dense as you can imagine (a serious mathematical text on a subject about which you know nothing). Ratings of 10 and above should be reserved for A-level texts and denser.

Choose a text around the 9 to 12 mark and skim the first few chapters, making a note of the parts you think you would need to read properly to get the gist.

Comment
You will be able to navigate (skimming and scanning) around lighter texts to save time to a greater or lesser degree: the denser the text, the greater the need to read it in a sequential fashion from beginning to end. There are more techniques for making sense of dense technical text in Chapter 5.

You can read books and attend lectures, but if the material genuinely extends your mathematical knowledge you are unlikely to understand or remember what you have read or heard unless you participate.

- To learn mathematics, it is necessary to *do* mathematics.

Ways of working on mathematics is the most important topic of the entire book and therefore has a whole chapter devoted to it (Chapter 6).

Some strategies you might find useful when doing mathematics:

- get an intuitive feel for something by 'playing' with it

- use sketches, diagrams and models to clarify your thinking

- make a conjecture about what is the case, i.e. an educated guess

- transfer ideas and methods from one situation to a slightly different situation

- test a statement or conjecture using examples

- prove a statement in an easy special case and then try to generalise this proof to cover all possible cases.

REFLECTION

Task 3.4 What next?

What are you going to do *now*, before moving on to the next chapter or section that you want to work on?

Comment
Here are some suggestions:

■ Look back at the list of diverse study activities given at the beginning of this chapter.
■ Reflect on what you have now learned or been reminded of (perhaps make a note of key points).
■ Decide on your priorities for the rest of this book, in order to make best use of the time that you have available.

- There are a variety of modes of study – the important thing with each is to be actively engaged.

- Most study activities will be enhanced by preparation beforehand.

- Developing effective note-making is useful for all modes of study.

- To learn mathematics, it is necessary to do mathematics.

- It is useful to reflect from time to time on whether you are making the best use of your study opportunities.

4

Assessment

This chapter is about how to plan, complete and benefit from the various forms of assessment. It contains practical hints and tips to help you approach coursework assignments and examinations positively and so produce your best work.

Initially, skim through this chapter so that you can return to the appropriate sections when they are relevant during your course. The first section is about assessment in general and then there are sections on continuous assessment (coursework assignments) and examinations.

ABOUT ASSESSMENT

The various forms of assessment are about monitoring how well you are doing towards achieving your aims and those of the course:

- for you to find out what you know and can do, so as to be able to plan the next stage of your studies (*formative* assessment)
- for the course authorities to judge what you know and can do against the criteria for the course: when you can demonstrate that you meet the learning outcomes, then you will qualify to go on to the next part of the course or be awarded a final qualification (*summative* assessment).

Formative assessment may be marked course preparatory assignments or informal tasks. For example:

- self-assessment, such as exercises or practice examination questions
- self-marked tests, exercises and examples set within the course.

Summative assessment is formal and subject to internal and external regulation. For example:

- graded tutor-marked coursework assignments that contribute to final grades (continuous assessment)
- examinable components.

All forms of assessment should contribute to your learning, although people sometimes tend to forget about the learning and think only about the formal assessment results. This is because of the natural concern to get good grades. But it is important that you keep reminding yourself about the learning. A lot of this chapter is about how to get as much as possible from assessment, in terms of extending what you know and what you can do.

Remember that your teachers, and those who designed and wrote your course, would like you to do well. It will not necessarily be easy for you and will involve sustained hard work. You need to plan well, use the help available and not lose heart. (If you do find that you seem to be on the wrong course, then discuss your problems with your tutor.)

How courses are formally assessed

Assessment of university courses or modules is by means of examination, coursework assignments or a mixture of both. You need to find out the assessment method for your course(s), because there are implications for the way in which you plan your study.

The various components may contribute varying proportions of the final grade, but it is usual to require a pass grade for each component. Some universities use first-year marks only to assess a student's eligibility to enter the second year.

CONTINUOUS ASSESSMENT

Throughout your course, you are likely to be set exercises, tasks or projects that you submit to your tutor or relevant lecturer.

What are assignments for?

Most courses have a number of course assignments, which you have to complete by set dates and then submit for marking. The grades you get for these will usually count towards your final course result. By doing assignments, you can:

- practise using skills and concepts introduced in your course
- consolidate areas of knowledge while they are still fresh in your mind
- reassure yourself that you are learning successfully
- assess the progress you have made.

Very importantly, you also receive *feedback*. When a marked assignment is returned to you, you have an opportunity to see if there are topics you have partly misunderstood or to learn about better ways of tackling a problem. By thinking these through, and acting on them, you are being an active learner. Your general grasp of the subject will be improved and you will be laying the groundwork for a good examination result.

You will also be learning more about *how to learn*. Being good at learning is a skill and, with practice, you can become better at it.

Figure 4.1 summarises how the assessment–feedback cycle leads to progress. A mistake that people sometimes make is to think that learning all goes on at stage 1. In fact, just as much learning usually happens during the other three stages. Each stage is important.

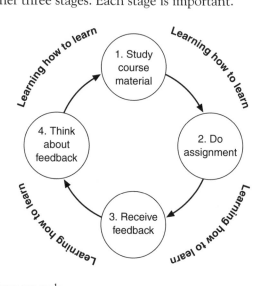

Figure 4.1 Assignment cycle.

Notice that this is part of the learning process and is helping you improve your ability to learn. So next time round the cycle, you will be a more skilful and experienced learner, the time after that better still, and so on.

Types of formal assessment

Assessment comes in a number of forms.

Tutor-marked assignments
Most courses require you to submit some form of written work to a tutor or lecturer, who will then mark it and provide suggestions and advice to help you.

Tutor-marked assignments offer you the chance to tackle questions that do not just have a single number or formula as the answer, but require a series of reasoned steps to arrive at a result.

The outstanding value of a tutor-marked assignment, to you as a learner, comes from the fact that a tutor can provide detailed comments on your individual performance, a sort of personal consultation, tailored for you. If feedback is too limited you may need to ask for more support.

Computer-marked assignments

There may also be assignments that are marked by computer. You write your answers on a special paper that can be read by optical reading devices or submit them directly online using a given template. Computer-marked assignments are well suited to multiple choice questions, where marking can easily be made automatic. Some computer marking systems generate automated feedback on the topics on which you need to do more work.

There are various forms of multiple choice questions. You should read the instructions and questions carefully. For some types of question, there is only one correct answer; for others, you need to select a number of correct solutions.

Preparatory assignments

Some courses have preparatory assignments. In some cases, there may be both tutor- and computer-marked ones. Preparatory assignments are not counted towards your final mark. They have two purposes:

- to give you feedback about how well prepared you are to start the course
- to let you practise submitting assignments before you have to do the real thing.

Preparatory assignments, although generally voluntary, are almost always worth bothering with. Even if you have mastered the requirements for starting the course, and fully understand procedures for submitting assignments, getting familiar with the routine will usually still pay dividends.

Electronic assignments

Some courses ask you to submit your tutor-marked assignments directly to your tutor in electronic form, using the Internet. This offers many advantages over submitting your work on paper: you do not need to worry that it will get lost in transit and the turnaround time can be reduced, because delivery is virtually instantaneous. However, unless you have your own computer, you need to make sure that you can get access to a computer in time to meet the cut-off date. (See Chapter 7 for possible problems with the electronic transfer of mathematical symbols.)

Group assignments

Sometimes an assignment can involve working on a problem with a group of fellow students. A proportion of the marks for the assignment may depend on this shared effort: for example, quality of oral presentation and/or written group report. Many people find their learning is improved by working with others. Moreover, problem-solving is often best approached as a team effort and is highly valued in the real world, so gaining skill at teamwork is valuable.

Assigned projects and portfolios
Some courses are assessed from portfolios, sometimes called an *end-of-course assessment* or ECA. This can be prepared over several weeks and may consist of explaining what you know about certain aspects of the course, together with evidence from activities and assignments done throughout the course.

On some courses, there is a final project. This will usually be the last assignment, or the last but one. Normally, it will count for more marks than an ordinary assignment. Projects may allow a topic to be explored in greater depth than would be possible otherwise. They may also allow ideas from different parts of the course to be brought together.

Planning and doing assignments

Each assignment will have a deadline. This is a date and time by which you are supposed to make sure your work has reached whoever is marking it (or feeding it into the computer). If you miss the deadline, and have not received permission to submit the assignment late, it is quite likely that it will not be marked and you may score zero for it.

Task 4.1 Why have deadlines?

List some reasons why assignments have deadlines and why it is important to meet them whenever possible.

Comment
It is important to meet deadlines whenever possible because:

- If you regularly let your deadlines slip, you may end up falling behind with the course.
- It is courteous to your tutor.
- Deadlines help to define the tempo of a course – they comprise the main mechanism to help students stay on schedule.
- While anybody was still doing the questions, it would be impossible to discuss the answers publicly – but learners often find group 'post-mortems' on an assignment very useful.
- Meeting deadlines is a valuable, transferable experience.

Most courses allow assignments to be sent after the deadline in exceptional circumstances, provided the extension has been authorised by the appropriate person. This could be your tutor or some other person in authority. You should find out the rules for your course, so that you know what to do should you have a problem.

Some courses don't in fact have any predetermined deadlines. It is up to each student to negotiate with his or her tutor when each assignment is due. So there are still deadlines, but they are not the same for all students.

Looking ahead

At the very beginning of the course, well before any assignments are due, you should check that you are sure of the answers to a number of practical matters. Here is a checklist.

- What sort of assignments does the course you are doing involve?
- How many are there of each kind?
- When are they due?
- What medium are they to be submitted in (on paper or electronically)?
- Where are they to be sent?
- Is there a covering form that you must send with each assignment you submit?
- Where will you find the questions?
- What are the arrangements if you need permission to submit an assignment late?

Mark assignments on a calendar
You will find it very useful to mark carefully the dates of the assignments you have to do on a calendar or planner, as well as other events in your course (any tutorials or day schools, broadcasts, the examination). You could also mark holidays, family events, periods when you expect your work to take up more time than usual and any other major time commitments that will potentially conflict with your assignments. This will mean that you will always be able to see at a glance what is coming next. You will be able to spot likely problems well in advance, while there is plenty of time to do something about them. And you will not miss any deadlines just because you forgot them.

Planning
It is likely that each assignment comprises several questions that match up in some way to the different topics covered in a particular section of the course. You should read quickly right through the question paper at the earliest possible opportunity. There is no need to worry about the detail at all at this stage. The objective is simply to give you a broad

overview, so that you have a feel for the questions you are going to have to answer. Then, as you study the material you can keep an eye open for areas that will be particularly useful for the assignment.

At what point should you begin doing the assignment? There are two main strategies.

1 Attempt each question immediately you have worked through the relevant material.
2 Work through all the material until all the studying is complete, then tackle all the questions one after another.

These are two very different ways of working. Surprisingly, there is little agreement about which is best, with many people coming down very strongly on one side or another.

Many people argue that Strategy 1 is best, because:

* it breaks up the task of doing the assignment
* having done Question 1, you have made obvious progress and can feel you have achieved something
* it is easier to answer a question on a topic when it is fresh in your mind.

This sounds very convincing. But others prefer Strategy 2. They argue that:

* completing a complete block of study before tackling the assignment means you have a far better overview of the relevant part of the course
* doing the whole assignment in one go saves having to keep going back to it repeatedly.

This sounds quite logical too. Of course, neither strategy is best for everyone. It really is a matter of personal preference. A compromise, or third strategy, might be to adopt Strategy 1 but only do 'in rough'; then go back over the whole lot once all the relevant study is completed, in order to produce the presentation to be submitted. This may take more time but is perhaps the best of both worlds.

* Find out which way of working suits you best.

Working on individual questions

Whichever strategy you adopt, the time will come when you sit down to answer Question 1.

Reading the question
First, decide on what the question is about and what you are being asked to do. Mathematics assignment and examination questions usually include particular instructional words that have specific meanings – these are 'doing' or 'process' words. There are categories of key words that can help in your decision on how to tackle the question and are worth highlighting when you see them in a question. However, you may need to interpret the precise meaning within the context of the specific question.

Some examples of process words and their implied meanings are:

- 'Write down', 'State', 'Give', 'Express/Express briefly', 'List', 'Specify' mean write down without justification, i.e. no working need be shown (although you may include appropriate working if it helps you).
- 'Find', 'Calculate', 'Determine', 'Simplify', 'Derive', 'Solve', 'Evaluate', 'Transform', 'Expand', 'Factorise', 'Differentiate', 'Integrate' mean work out and show your working, using standard results and techniques.
- 'Prove', 'Show', 'Deduce', 'Explain', 'Indicate', 'Justify', 'Demonstrate', 'Determine', 'Decide (if, whether …)', 'Verify', 'Confirm', 'Test', 'Predict', 'Illustrate', 'Identify' mean you must justify each step and provide a convincing argument.
- 'Assume', 'Consider', 'Suppose', 'Apply', 'Use', 'Define (in terms of …)', 'Sketch', 'Draw', 'Plot', 'Graph', 'Compile (a table, …)', 'Make (a table, list, …)' indicate you must answer the question in a particular way indicated by whatever words immediately follow each of these cueing terms.
- 'Explore', 'Investigate', 'Devise', 'Design', 'Obtain', 'Find', 'Adapt', 'Construct', 'Produce (an algorithm, argument, diagram, …)', 'Translate (from, into, …)' indicate doing a mathematical activity and then reporting on the process and result.
- 'Submit (a printout, list, …)', 'Include', 'Supply', 'Provide', 'Attach' mean you need to provide evidence of having used something, for example a particular software package.

Working on the problem
Having decided what the question is about, it is extremely unlikely that you will be able to work smoothly through it from beginning to end at the first attempt. Most people work in a much messier way. You will almost certainly:

- have to keep checking back through the course material and notes
- take a wrong turning and have to backtrack
- get stuck at some point
- find your approach is wrong somewhere
- feel tired and frustrated at some stage.

All this is quite normal. Even professional mathematicians meet numerous obstacles and setbacks. But when their work is written up and published, all that is forgotten. The final product all looks so perfect, as if the author just dashed it all straight off. The reality is no one can do mathematics without getting their hands dirty, so to speak. So expect the process to be messy, but do not let that put you off.

At this stage, you will be concentrating mostly on working out the mathematics of your answer. Its final presentation is important, but you can worry about the detail of that later. So you might write quite rough notes, that only you understand, and include information that will not appear in the final answer, but which helps you to think about the problem as you work on it.

You are not alone

When you hand your written work in, it must all have come from you and no one else. But this does not mean you cannot get help when you are finding out how to do the questions. Discussion with fellow students is all right so long as it is before you write your answers. Here are some sources of assistance with ideas and techniques.

Other students

Other students are a valuable learning resource. Together you can discuss course material and tease out its meaning. Just knowing that other students have difficulty with the same topics as you can be tremendously reassuring. Discussion can be face-to-face, on the telephone, by e-mail or may take place on an electronic conference.

It is alright to talk to other students about many aspects of an assignment, such as:

- what you believe a question or a part of a question is asking for
- what sections of the course you think are relevant
- what other sources of information you have found for this area
- ways of tackling the question.

Often, you can also draw a lot of comfort from talking to fellow students about how well you feel you are progressing with the assignment and which parts of it you are finding the most challenging. But you should never exchange your actual notes or answers with others.

- Remember that the answers you eventually hand in must be all your own work, however much you have discussed the questions with other people.

Your tutor or lecturer
Your tutor obviously cannot tell you any of the solutions until after the assignment has been marked. But that does not mean she or he cannot help you, perhaps providing you with useful guidance, without giving anything away about the answers. Your tutor may be able to clarify the wording or point you to an example that shows what level of detail is expected in the answer. It is perfectly legitimate for you to seek advice of this kind, to make sure that you have properly understood what is being asked of you.

Books, web sites, and so on
If you put something into your assignment that is not your own words, but a direct quotation from somewhere else, you need to acknowledge your source.

Other people
You may have informed friends or colleagues (or even family) you can ask for assistance. It is all right to do so, but do not forget that:

- they must not do bits of your assignment for you: they can help you understand the ideas, and give advice, but the answers have to come from you
- if you ask them too often they will soon get fed up – make sure that they do not mind and try to keep your enquiries to a minimum.

Plagiarism
Many institutions have explicit plagiarism contracts. You must not pass off other people's work as your own. Plagiarism normally carries stiff penalties.

Putting your assignment together

Answering or solving the assignment questions is not the final stage. Your assignment needs to be submitted and in a form that is clear and understandable to the person marking it.

Audience
When you write your assignment, remember you have an audience. Mathematics is a subject where it is tempting to write everything in note form, but this is not good communication. Your purpose is to demonstrate to the marker what you know. It makes it much easier for a reader to follow what you are saying if you write in complete, logical sentences.

Keep to the layout of the question paper
An assignment will have several questions. These are often broken down into a number of smaller parts.

When you come to answer the questions, it is quite possible that for various reasons you do not attempt them in exactly the same order as they are written. No problem. But before you hand your work in, always tidy it up, so questions and answers both come in precisely the same order.

If an assignment is to be submitted in electronic form, you will often be given a *template*, which you must use, comprising a file with spaces for you to fill in the answers.

Task 4.2 Why does layout matter?

Think of some reasons why it is very important to stick to the layout given in the question paper.

Comment
If you stick to the layout, there is much less chance that you will overlook part of a question. It will be easy to check it is all there. It will help your tutor follow your answers. When you come to revise, you will certainly want to look back over your assignment work, so be sure to make it easy to follow.

In some assignments, a small number of marks are set aside for good presentation – including labelling diagrams, writing in sentences and giving units of measure, if relevant. This is because communicating with others is a vital part of doing mathematics. It is no good being a genius if nobody else can understand you.

Key points to check before submission
- *Say who you are*. Make certain you write your name on every sheet of paper you use. You may have a personal identifier or number: if so, you should write that too. If your work is not easily identifiable, it could get mixed up with someone else's.
- *Number the pages*. It is also a good idea to say how many pages there are altogether, numbering them, for example, 1/9, 2/9, 3/9 or whatever the total number of pages is. That way it is possible to see at a glance if your work is all there.
- *Two sides to every story*. Sometimes your tutor may ask you to write on one side of the page only, so she or he will have somewhere to write if necessary. Or you may choose yourself to write only on the front of each sheet of paper. If you do write only on the front of each sheet,

stick to this all the way through. Whatever you do, leave plenty of space for your tutor's comments.

- *If you missed something, say why.* That way your tutor will know that the answer has not just got lost in transit. If you do not understand something, say what it is. This makes it much easier for your tutor to help you.
- *Label diagrams.* You should make sure diagrams are labelled and appear at the right place in the answer. If this is not possible, make sure that you include a reference to where the particular diagram may be found (e.g. write 'See appendix 1').
- *State units.* You should give the units of physical quantities. For example, write 3 years, 15 kg, 42 mm and not just 3, 15 or 42 as an answer. If you miss off the units, the reader will not know whether you are measuring time in millennia or microseconds.
- *Final check.* Somebody has to read what you have written. When you have finished writing an assignment, go away and leave it for a while. Then come back and imagine another person wrote it, and that you are reading it for the first time. Are all symbols written clearly and used correctly? Which parts are hard to follow? Can you see some small changes that will make the whole thing easier to understand? Do not waste too much time going over and over what you have done – one check is normally sufficient.
- *Keep a copy.* If your assignment is on paper, you should ideally keep a spare copy. At the very least, you should keep all your notes. It is very rare indeed for assignments to go missing, but it is not impossible. If your assignment was done on a computer, make a back-up copy and store it in a safe place.

All about marks

Most people feel a lot more vulnerable about the marks they get for academic work than they would about how they did in a pub quiz or a football game. Not getting high marks can touch a nerve.

From time to time, you may meet some sort of problem: illness or a personal difficulty at home or work. You may have to travel for work or be on holiday. There could be a bit of the course you just do not get on with. If this happens, you may be tempted not to submit the assignment at all, if you feel that you have not had time to do it properly. This is a mistake – better a low mark than zero.

- Hand in every assignment, however little of it you have done.

The reasons for this are:

- Assignments are as much about learning as they are about grades – if you do not submit a piece of work, you will miss out on the feedback from your tutor.
- Any mark is always better than no marks. Non-submissions may count against you in any performance review.

Substitution
On many courses there is a compensation or substitution rule, designed to minimise the impact of a single bad mark in a run of better ones. So find out what the rules are for your course.

How to get as many marks as possible
Before you start each question, ask yourself 'What is this question about?'. This can usually be expressed in a single sentence, which will tie in with the learning outcomes for the course. For example, 'Can the student use a linear recurrence relation to model a simple financial problem?'.

So each question has a definite objective. If you can work out the theme of the question, it is bound to help. Being able to see the purpose of the question provides you with a compass that will help you stay on track. You will be able to tell you are going in the right direction. If you have to consult the course material, you will have useful clues about where to look.

Mark allocation
You will sometimes be told how many marks are allocated to each part of a question. This is important information.

Task 4.3 What's it worth?

What sort of things would you take into account if you were trying to decide how many marks to allocate to a part of a question? Take 5 minutes to jot down as many as you can think of. When you have finished, see if you agree with the factors listed below.

Comment
These are the factors that are usually taken into account when deciding how many marks to allocate to part of a question:

- how many steps the solution requires
- how much time and effort it is likely to take
- the number of new or difficult ideas involved
- whether the solution is very different from worked examples in the course material.

It can be important to take note of the mark allocation, for the following reasons:

- First, it is a guide to how much time and effort you should expect to spend on that part of the assignment. Imagine a part is only worth two marks. Then you would not expect to take a whole evening over it or to have to write several pages. If you do, you are either providing far too much detail or you have missed the point of the question somewhere. On the other hand, if a part is worth 20 marks, you would not suppose it can be answered as a one-liner you can write in 30 seconds.
- Second, it may give a clue about how many items the answer is supposed to contain. This does not always work, but if a question reads, 'List the reasons why … [3]', it is worth wondering if there could be three reasons listed in the marking schedule.

Do not lose marks unnecessarily
It is very easy and very common for marks to be lost for causes that are completely avoidable. These are marks that you should have got, but did not. So when you get the results back, you feel a bit like kicking yourself.

Make sure you have done what the question actually asks and not what you *think* it asks.

Here are four top tips for not throwing marks away needlessly.

1 *Read the small print and do what it asks.* If a question wants an answer correct to 3 significant figures, then give 3 significant figures. Count significant figures and not decimal places. Do not give 2, 4 or some other number. (If you are not given advice on accuracy, use what is sensible and state the accuracy you have chosen and possibly the reason for your choice.) If it tells you to state any general rules you have used, then state them. Sometimes a question (or even a whole assignment) may begin with an instruction that you are asked to follow throughout. Later on, it is easy to forget this instruction, so perhaps highlight or underline it.

2 *Answer the whole question.* Questions often come with an extra little bit tacked on at the end. This is easily overlooked. What probably happens is that you are very focused on the main part of the question. When you finish that, you feel a strong sense of completion and do not think to go back and check that you have actually done everything.

3 *Check numbers very carefully.* Everybody knows how easy it is to make mistakes when copying numbers. For example, 13562 can easily get transcribed as 13652.

4 *Show working.* When there are several marks for a question, you will nearly always get some credit for a partially correct answer. But if you show no working, just an incorrect final figure, it is impossible for your

tutor to give you any marks at all. Worse than that, they will not be able to tell where you went wrong, so they cannot provide the best possible feedback.

Submitting your assignment
Check that:

- your answer is all there – you have not overlooked any of the pages
- you are submitting it to the right place, especially if this is the first assignment you have done
- you have filled in any covering form correctly
- if you are sending the assignment by mail, you have paid the right postage (underpayment may cause a delay at the other end and tutors are not known for being happy to pay excess postage for the privilege of receiving your work to mark).

What to do when you get your assignment back

When it arrives back, the first thing you are likely to think about is the mark or grade you received. You may feel quite anxious about this. After all, you have probably put a great deal of time and effort into your work, so it is natural to worry about how it will be judged. (One student remarked she wished the return envelope could be marked 'Safe to open'.)

If you got a lot less than you hoped for, you may feel hurt or angry. Such emotions are quite normal, but if you can you should try not to let them stop you being an effective learner.

If you experience very strong feelings, it may be a good idea to put the assignment aside for a while, until you feel in a more positive frame of mind. But try hard not to simply pigeonhole it indefinitely, because if you do you will miss out on opportunities for learning. It is a cliché, but still true nevertheless, that nobody ever learned anything worthwhile without making quite a few mistakes along the way.

Most tutors think of themselves first and foremost as teachers. Your tutor will have looked very carefully at what you have done and may have written detailed, individual feedback for you, designed to help in various ways, perhaps including:

- explanations of key points that you may have misunderstood slightly, starting from your own work and leading you through the solution
- suggestions about sections of course material you might just want to brush up on quickly
- advice about topics to concentrate on
- sample solutions and hints about how to present answers
- general tips about approaches to study
- extensions to the original question that you may find interesting.

The best way to make use of this feedback is to read it fairly soon after you get it, while the subject of the assignment is still fresh in your mind. First, read any overall comments at the front or end. Then, run through your script, noting the suggestions your tutor has offered. You may like to write a very short summary to remind you of the key points – many learners find this useful. Try to decide if there are any important lessons that you should bear in mind when you do your next assignment. Remember, like all learning, this is an active process – it is not something being done to you, but you yourself getting to grips with what your tutor has written.

You should not take too long over this assignment review – as little as 20 minutes could be enough. Many students also look over past assignments when they come to prepare for the examination. It helps remind them of important facts and techniques, pitfalls to avoid, levels of detail expected and how to lay answers out. So having studied the feedback, put the assignment away somewhere you will be able to find it again later.

Your tutor may have invited you to contact him or her further if you have any questions or if you are still having trouble with a topic. It they have written this, it means they are anxious to help you get a clear grasp of the material concerned *before* you go on to the next bit of study and you should not feel embarrassed about taking them up on the offer if you need to. Most tutors would far rather you contacted them than struggled on your own.

Task 4.4 Review

Now imagine that the last subsection, 'What to do when you get your assignment back', was actual advice from your tutor. Read through it again and try to summarise the main points.

Comment
This task involved you practising reading some suggestions and noting down the main points. Look back at what you wrote. Do you feel you picked up all the main things? Will you be able to follow your notes in (say) 6 months' time? If not, how can you make them clearer?

The marking scheme
The course you are taking will probably have a large team of tutors teaching it. To ensure that the marks awarded by different tutors are comparable, there is likely to be a common marking scheme that they must all work to. Having a marking scheme also helps to ensure that all

students are marked consistently and fairly. When you are looking through your returned assignment, remember that the marks your tutor has given you will be dictated to a considerable extent by the marking scheme.

Within the marking scheme, tutors do have some scope for flexibility and if they are in doubt they will usually be generous.

If you believe your mark is wrong
If you think your tutor has made a genuine mistake, you should contact him or her at the earliest opportunity. Explain exactly what you believe is wrong. Say precisely what the mistake you think you have found is, where it is and how many marks are involved. If your tutor has not got a copy of your answer, send one, so they can see what you are referring to. If there has been a mistake, tutors will usually be only too glad to put the record straight.

Keep going

If you get one or two relatively poor marks, do not assume you will fail the course. Check what marks you have got so far, what the rules are and what you need to pass. You will almost certainly be surprised. It is quite common for students to believe there is no hope and give up, when there is still plenty of opportunity to do enough to pass the course. In some cases, they may have already done enough to pass, but just not realised it.

- If you are even vaguely considering giving up, talk to your tutor – who will be able to give you sound advice applicable to your circumstances.

EXAMINATIONS

This section is about taking examinations and how you can prepare for them efficiently and thoroughly. Topics are included on:

- making the best use of revision time
- strategies for achieving your best
- ways of reducing the anxiety that often surrounds examinations.

Why examinations are necessary

Here are some possible reasons:

- Examinations are often compulsory if you want to count your learning towards a qualification.

- Passing the examination shows that you have studied the material to the required depth.
- Revising and sitting an examination helps you to bring the different elements of the course together.
- A student *could* cheat by having excessive help with assignments during their study of the course – but they are then unlikely to know enough to pass the examination.
- In an examination, you can show that you can perform satisfactorily under pressure.

Bringing together the different elements of the course
One result of successful revision and examination performance is that you are able to see how the whole course fits together. Each section of a course is often studied in isolation; once an assignment has been completed, that block can get forgotten when you start the next. During your revision, the connections between different parts of the course become clearer, and this should aid your understanding of the material and as a whole help you to remember the important facts and techniques during the examination itself.

Performing for yourself and the examiner
There are many jobs where it is crucial that you are able to perform successfully under pressure. This is one of the reasons why many courses leading to qualifications have terminal examinations. During an examination, you are showing the examiner that:

- you have learned the important facts and techniques taught in the course
- you are able to bring together coherently many of the elements of the course
- you can apply the facts and techniques to new situations
- you can perform successfully under stress.

Examiners know that the scripts they mark were produced under stressful conditions – they have all been there before. Examination papers are not designed to trip you up, but to help you demonstrate your knowledge. Examiners will do their best to give you the marks you deserve.

Planning your revision

Revision needs to be planned:

- to ensure that everything necessary is revised
- to revise effectively and efficiently
- to fit in revision around other commitments.

When to start revising

Some students leave their revision until the last few days, while others start after the first week of the course. There is no 'right' time to start revising – it depends on your personal commitments, on your preferred method of studying, on whether you just want a pass or are aiming for a top grade. What is important is that you start *thinking* about revision earlier rather than later. What you need to do is to work out how much time you have available and then plan your revision around it.

Making a revision timetable

Now that you have started thinking about revising, you should be ready to make your revision timetable. The notes below will help you do this.

1 Decide when you are going to start and work out how long that gives you. (Are some weeks more heavily committed than others?) Start as early as possible – do not leave it until the last minute.
2 Decide what to cover, in what depth and when. This needs careful thought and as much advice as you can get. Which resources do you have available? Which are you going to use?
3 Match up your time to revise with the material to revise and plan a timetable that is realistic.
4 Use a revision timetable to plan the last few weeks leading up to the examination(s). Put on the date and session of each examination. Date the weeks leading up to the examination(s). Add in work, family and social commitments.
5 In the early weeks, plan to study material you have not completed and make time to do any final assignments.
6 Leave the last week for concentrated revision or consolidation, covering all of the topics you have identified as important.
7 Use the day before the examination to gather examination materials and prepare for the journey, etc.

Updating your plans

The timetable you have created for yourself is not set in stone – you will probably find that you will be continually updating it, either because your revision of a particular topic has not gone as you expected or because outside constraints have resulted in changes. However, if you are continually reorganising your plans, you may need to consider whether you are setting yourself targets that are too demanding.

Task 4.5 An outline revision timetable

Fill in your timetable by indicating which block, unit or topic you plan to revise in each section of the timetable (you may need to adapt it to suit your own circumstances).

Outline revision timetable

Weeks to exam		MON	TUE	WED	THUR	FRI	SAT	SUN
6	a.m.							
	p.m.							
	evening							
5	a.m.							
	p.m.							
	evening							
4	a.m.							
	p.m.							
	evening							
3	a.m.							
	p.m.							
	evening							
2	a.m.							
	p.m.							
	evening							
1	a.m.							
	p.m.							
	evening							

Comment

Does your timetable look realistic? Have you allowed time for unexpected events to happen? Will you have enough time to cover everything in detail? If not, you will either have to try to find more time or decide which blocks, units or topics to spend more time on.

Task 4.6 When should you stop revising?

Make some notes giving your thoughts on when you ought to *stop* revising.

Comment
You might have included the following points:

- when you feel tired
- when you know that you are not taking in any more information
- it might be better to do no revision on the day before the examination – that way, you will be fresher when it matters, namely when you are actually doing the examination.

Revision resources

You are likely to have a large amount of material that, by this stage of your study, may well be all mixed up. Before you decide which resources you are going to use, you might find it useful to sort it out into course units, assignments, supplementary material, your own notes, tutorial notes, etc.

Past and specimen examination papers
One of your first tasks should be to look at past and specimen examination papers, to find out what their formats are. If the examination paper turns out not to be what you expect, you will be at an important disadvantage right from the start. Some of the things you need to find out about the paper are listed on the opposite page.

Formula sheets and handbooks
In some mathematics courses, formula sheets or handbooks can be used during the examination. Formula sheets are provided with the examination paper (there should be a copy with any specimen paper); handbooks are provided as part of the course material. You need to know whether such aids are permitted in the examination and whether they may be annotated beforehand.

Revision techniques

Remember that this is *revision* – it is unlikely that you will have time to redo the course, read all or some of the course material or do some or all of the exercises and activities in the course. Remember, as well, that revision should be active – you need to be *doing* things throughout your revision.

Question	Your answer
How much time do you have to do the examination?	
Is the paper divided into sections?	
Are there compulsory questions or sections?	
How many questions are there?	
How many questions do you have to answer?	
Do the questions require short or long answers?	
How are the questions arranged on the page?	
Do you do your answers on the question paper or in a separate answer book?	
How are the questions weighted in terms of marks?	
Are there any multiple-choice questions?	
How much time should you allow for each question or section?	
Do questions relate to particular parts of the course (units, blocks, books) or do they relate to the key course themes?	
Does the language in the questions seem familiar?	
Are there any questions that draw on pre-release material?	
Can you take any material, such as course material or a handbook, into the exam? Can this material be annotated?	
Are formula sheets available?	
Is a calculator permitted and, if so, what type?	
If you cannot find out the answers, ask your tutor or another staff member.	

Task 4.7 What revision techniques do you already know?

Write down the revision techniques for mathematics you have found useful in the past and any that you have already thought of for your next examination.

Revision techniques

Comment

You could have written down one or more of the following techniques listed:

- list the assessable topics (learning outcomes) and study relevant material again
- work through relevant activities, examples, problems, proofs
- course mapping, to get an overall view of the course
- make spray diagrams linking major concepts
- condense the notes you made during the course into briefer ones
- summarise the important ideas and techniques
- work with other students to prepare summaries of the important topics
- prepare notes to teach a topic to your fellow students
- analyse questions from the examiner's perspective
- do questions from past and specimen papers
- do one of the past papers or the specimen paper under examination conditions.

Don't worry if you fail to recognise some of the above methods – the next few pages will go into them in detail. You will need to decide which technique (or techniques) are suitable for the particular course you are currently revising for – some may be more appropriate than others.

Your revision is likely to be more effective if, from time to time, you vary the activities you undertake: for example, answering specific questions, general reading, summarising topics, etc. Have frequent breaks, to avoid getting tired.

Course mapping
Many ideas and techniques taught throughout your course will be linked
– for example, you would find the ideas behind calculus almost impossible to understand if you did not already know some algebra. You might
find it useful to get an overall view of the course by drawing a diagram
showing how the different blocks are connected to each other.

Condensing your notes
If you made notes during your original study of the course, you could
condense them down until you have one A4 page for each topic. While
you are doing this, you are focusing on the main themes and techniques
of the topic. As your revision progresses, you could condense your notes
even further, finally to a small index card with the key ideas such as definitions, techniques, notation, worked examples, conjectures, proofs,
exceptions, formulae and rules.

Task 4.8 Condensing

Try this method for one of the main topics in your present (or previous)
course.

Comment
If you find this very time-consuming then this may not be an effective
method for you. In part, it will depend on the type of material you are
working with.

Using assignments to make summaries
Assignment questions can be a good indicator of examination questions,
as they are usually intended to bring out the important points of each
topic or section of your course. For each assignment question, compare it
with the relevant examination questions on past papers and ask yourself
the following questions:

• How do the questions differ?
• What is the key difference between the answers on an assignment
  question and on an examination paper?

When you have answered the above questions, you could make a short
summary of the key points, formulae and techniques for each topic.

Task 4.9 Make a summary

Choose a topic, compare assignment and examination questions and then produce a summary.

Comment
In some courses, the examination questions are more straightforward than the corresponding assignment questions and so less detail will probably be needed. If you do have the time, you could redo the assignment questions and compare your answers with those you did initially and with any comments from your tutor.

Working with other students
If you are able to attend tutorials, you should already have found that discussion among students is one of the easiest ways of learning. The following list gives some ideas of how tutorials or self-help group sessions can help you to revise:

- Discuss revision techniques you have found helpful in the past.
- Share your assignment answers on particular topics and note any different methods of tackling questions.
- Compare your condensed notes with those from other students – you may all have missed some important points.
- If your examination involves essay writing, have a short 'brainstorming' session on planning the answer to a particular question.

Teach a topic
This is another idea for tutorials or self-study groups, although it needs more pre-planning than the others. The method involves you choosing a topic that you think you know well, preparing some notes on it and then teaching it to your tutorial group. A question-and-answer session afterwards will reveal gaps in your (and their) knowledge.

Task 4.10 Learning by teaching

Prepare teaching notes on a topic you are familiar with and, if possible, carry it out.

Comment
Even if you are unable actually to do the teaching, make teaching notes is a good way of focusing your revision.

Using a handbook
You should already know whether you can take a handbook into your examination and whether it can be annotated or not. If a handbook is allowed, you need to use it right from the start of your revision, so that the layout and contents become familiar. Knowing that you could find a particular technique or concept in your handbook during the examination is often enough to allay much of the anxiety you may feel about 'freezing up'. You may not use the handbook at all in the examination, but you have the reassurance of knowing it is there if you should need it. Indeed, learning what is in your handbook (and why these and not other things have been included) is a useful form of revision in itself.

You will need to find out how much annotation is allowed from the instructions for your examination. This can be:

- no annotation permitted
- limited annotation (highlighting, underlining) allowed
- limited comments can be made in the margins
- limited comments and outline answers to questions allowed
- no limit on the amount that can be written in the handbook, but no extra pages or tabs allowed.

Know your calculator
As with your handbook, you need to know whether a calculator can be taken into the examination and, if so, if there is any restriction on the type of calculator that can be used. This information should be given in your examination instructions. This is something you need to know as early as possible, so that you are familiar with the model allowed and can use it throughout your revision.

Using past papers
Doing questions from past papers is very useful as part of your revision. You do need to have used one or more of the revision methods detailed above before you look at past papers – it can be very demoralising to look through a past paper early on in your revision and discover that you cannot do any of the questions. Also, past papers can usually only be taken as a *guide* to the type and level of questions to be expected, not the exact content. (Beware of changes in syllabus or approach. Many institutions do not provide answers to past papers and very few provide specimen papers.)

Start by concentrating on the questions from one section or even one topic:

- Try the questions on one of the past papers on the topic, using your handbook if necessary to look up any formulae – check your answers against those provided by the examiners or your tutor.

- Make notes on questions or parts of questions you could not answer.
- Use your course material to revise the material you did not know.
- Try a similar question on a different past paper.

Sometimes the questions on a particular topic are quite similar (perhaps just with different numbers) on the papers from different years. Attempt the different types of questions for each topic using the above method, but try to leave some unanswered until later.

Once you feel that you have revised the entire course, do most of the rest of the questions from past papers (or even repeat those you attempted earlier). You should try to leave one paper (maybe the specimen) to do under examination conditions.

At this stage, you should be trying not only to answer the questions correctly, but to do so quickly as well.

Doing a mock examination

At some point during your revision, preferably near to the real examination (but not so near that you do not have any time to brush up on important topics you still need to revise further), you should try to do a full examination paper under examination conditions. (You should work through the next subsection in this chapter on preparing for the examination *before* you attempt a mock examination.)

Ensure that you have the required time without being disturbed, that you have all of the necessary equipment and that you are not too exhausted after all the time you have spent on your revision. Do the examination in the way you hope to do it for real, and try not to panic – remember that this is not the real examination and you still have time for some further revision.

Mark your answers afterwards and try to assess your performance.

Last-minute revision

If you find that your revision plan has had to be adjusted, and you have run out of time, remind yourself of the contents of a topic by flicking through your notes, reading course material, looking at assignments, etc.

Preparing for the examination

Understand the language

Mathematics assignment and examination questions usually include words that have different meanings when compared with their day-to-day usage. These are most often 'doing' or 'process' words (discussed earlier in this chapter in the section on working on individual questions).

Task 4.11 Process words in your examination

Look through your past and specimen examination papers and note the use of process words (p. 49) and any others that seem to determine what you are being asked to do (these words are usually verbs in the imperative).

Comment
If you found other process words in the papers, the detail in the answers might indicate their meaning. If you are still unsure, you could ask your tutor for clarification.

Practise your handwriting

This is important, particularly if you have word processed your tutor-marked assignments. Unless you have special needs that allow you to use a word processor in the examination, you will need to be able to write quickly and legibly and for 2 or 3 hours at a time. As part of your revision, practise writing as fast and as legibly as you can for longer and longer periods each day. There is little point in getting everything correct on your examination paper if the markers are unable to read what you have written.

Essential materials

What must you have to hand for the examination?

Task 4.12 What to take into the examination

Make a list of the items you think you ought to take with you into the examination.

Comment
Your list must contain the items below:

- pens, pencils, ruler, eraser
- a calculator (if allowed)
- your handbook (if allowed)
- examination number and proof of identification.

It may also include these items:
- other mathematical equipment, such as a protractor and compass
- essential medication (e.g. for hay fever)
    - drinks, sweets and other suitable refreshments
    - tissues.

The week before
You should start your physical preparations for the actual examination
during the week before.

Task 4.13 The week before

Check items in the following list for your examination, adding any others
you can think of.

What is the day, date and time of your examination?	
Where is the examination centre?	
How are you going to get there?	
How long will it take you?	
If you are going by car, where is the nearest available parking and what if it turns out to be full?	
If you are going by public transport, where is the nearest stop to the examination centre and how reliable is the timetable?	
Do you need to make arrangements such as childcare or permission for leave from work?	
Do you need to buy any equipment to take into the examination?	
Does your calculator need new batteries? (if you are not sure, fit new ones anyway)	

Comment
It would be dreadful if you missed the examination because you had
misread the examination timetable or if the batteries ran out on your calculator halfway through. Checking things in good time before the examination
removes one cause of stress.

The day before
There are many things you could do on the day before the examination
– sleep, do some physical activity, skim through your revision notes for
reassurance, collect everything you need.

The day of the examination
You need to ensure that the period of time before your examination
starts is as stress-free as possible. This might mean that you:

- arrive at the centre in good time
- have thought about what you are going to do if you arrive very early
- have checked what you can do if there is an unexpected problem.

Unexpected problems
Students sometimes face unexpected problems that either severely
decrease their performance in the examination or even prevent them
from taking it. The following list gives just some examples of problems
that could arise:

- you become ill during the examination
- you become ill before the examination
- you are involved in an accident
- your car or bus or train breaks down
- there is a family crisis.

Task 4.14 What should you do if the unexpected happens?

Find out what provision is made for the sort of circumstances outlined
above. This information is likely to be found in the instructions given to you
ahead of the examination.

Comment
The institution and/or examiners cannot do anything about your problem if
they do not know about it.

Therefore, if you are taken ill during the examination, let the invigilator
know immediately, and, if necessary, ask to be taken out of the examination room under supervision. Whether or not you can finish the examination, ask the invigilator to send in a report on your illness and also send a
letter yourself. If possible, get a medical certificate to include with your
application for special consideration.

In the other situations, you might be better not taking the examination,
particularly if there is provision for an alternative examination soon after
the date of the original one. You will need to contact the organisers of your
examination as soon as possible and certainly within a few days, explaining the problem. Your initial contact would need to be followed up by docu-
mentary evidence, such as a medical certificate.

Doing the examination

Getting started

The hardest part of any examination is getting started. Students have failed exams because they spent the first 20 minutes staring at the (usually straightforward) first question; the panic rises and they then have the same problem with the next question.

There are some tasks you should do at the very start of the examination, before you start answering any questions. These are:

- Read the instructions on the front, making a note of compulsory questions and choices of question.
- Skim read through the whole paper.
- If there is a choice, make an initial choice of questions.
- Plan a rough order in which to do the questions.

Managing your time

You are more likely to pass the examination if you choose the questions to do carefully and spend the first few minutes of the examination in planning your time and your answers. The following provides some suggestions, particularly for examinations that have several sections where you need to choose questions from each section.

Choose the questions and order them:

- during your first read through of the paper, tick those questions you feel confident about
- read through the questions you have ticked and put an additional tick against the ones you prefer
- start by answering the questions with the most ticks.

When planning to use the time available, you should:

- make sure that you are answering the right number of questions and the right number from each section
- divide your time according to the number of marks for each question and/or section
- write down the optimum finishing time for each question
- try to allow 10 minutes for checking at the end.

Try to stick to your plan; if you do end up with less time to do the last question, plan your answer and write out the main points in note form. This could earn you a few marks.

Plan your answers:

- mark the key words in the question
- mark the process words to help you understand the instructions within the question.

How to pass the examination
Here is one method for tackling mathematics examinations that is applicable to those examinations where all (or most) of the questions are compulsory.

1 Get started, by choosing an easy question i.e. one that is easy for you.
2 Now that your confidence is starting to increase, go through the paper, doing those questions you feel confident about tackling. (You will probably get enough marks to pass during this first part of the examination.)
3 Once you have been through the paper once, start again at the beginning, tackling those questions you had left which now, with your increased confidence, seem to be more straightforward. (Still leave the ones that you are not confident of tackling – you cannot afford to sit and stare at a question for 10 minutes while there are still questions you can do in less time.)
4 Keep an eye on the time – if you are spending too long on one question, cut your losses and move on.
5 Check your answers:
   • Have you answered the questions you are given, rather than the ones you would like to have been given?
   • Have you made any obvious mistakes (e.g. inappropriate rounding)?
   • Have you missed out part of a question by mistake?
6 Now, if there is still time, go back to the questions you have not done – once you have tackled every question you feel confident about, then there is nothing lost by spending 10 minutes on a question you are quite unsure about.

Coping with any anxiety
As the examination date approaches, you may be getting anxious about it, even if you feel that you have revised thoroughly. The tension created by anxiety may make you sleep less. Use this time productively – do some extra, though perhaps less intensive, revision, go for a walk or use some relaxation techniques. Almost any practical activity will help to reduce the tension. You need to practise techniques for managing your anxiety from whenever you start your revision.

The exercises below are ones that you can do at any time, during your revision as well as the examination. They can help to allay the panic and the increase in tension.

1 *The 'Stop' method.* Tell yourself to 'STOP' (out loud, unless you are actually in the examination room). Sit back in your seat and relax, with your arms hanging loose. Curl and uncurl your fingers to let the tension drain from them. After 10 or 20 seconds, continue with what you were doing.

2 *Breathing*. Stop what you are doing and concentrate on your breathing. Then breathe in through your nose and exhale slowly through your mouth – try to imagine that you are blowing away your anxiety. Repeat this a few times before starting back to work.

Task 4.15 Try them out

During your revision, if you start to feel over-anxious try one of the methods above.

Comment

During your revision, practise both methods and any others you already know, in order to work out what is the best way for you to control any anxiety.

Self-talk: turn negative statements into positive ones
If you feel that your anxiety is caused by a lack of self-confidence, a technique called 'self-talk' is one that some people find useful. You can guide your thinking away from the negative feelings of general anxiety and self-doubt by turning negative self-statements into more positive ones. The example in Table 4.1 illustrates the process (adapted from The Open University toolkit on revision and examinations).

Table 4.1 Self-talk

Negative self-talk	Positive self-talk
I'm hopeless at examinations and I always let myself down.	I'm working well and I'm planning to use techniques that will help.
I always leave revision until the last minute and then panic.	I have a revision plan that I'll stick to.
I might fail.	I'm determined to pass and I'm working hard enough to make that happen.

After the examination

Have you thought about what you will do as soon as the examination is finished and later, when you are waiting for the results?

It is not usually a good idea to discuss the examination in detail with other students straight afterwards – if you have got answers different from someone else, you will probably worry and you cannot do anything about it at this stage. It is also not useful to do the examination again outside of the examination room, for similar reasons. You need to forget about the examination and do something completely different, something you did not have the time for before – treat yourself.

How you have performed

Do not expect to get as many marks in the examination as you did on assignments – you can spend hours and hours on an assignment question that you only had 20 minutes for in the examination. If you have revised thoroughly and effectively, and you did not make a complete mess of the examination, you will almost certainly have passed. If not, most universities allow retakes of intermediate examinations.

- Assignments are as much about learning as they are about grades.

- Try to present your assignments in an organised and clear form.

- Try to make sure you have not thrown marks away because of silly mistakes.

- When you get your assignment back, spend some time reflecting on the feedback you have received.

- Start thinking about examination revision early in the course.

- Use a variety of activities during revision.

- Do not give up – keep going. Success is usually due in large measure to determination and perseverance.

5

Mathematical communication

This chapter is about mathematical communication in speech and text, using words and symbols, and is also about various forms of visual representations, including diagrams and graphs. It includes discussion of both speaking and writing about mathematical activity, and considers the purposes and audiences for which mathematical work is produced, as well as the conventions used. It will help you to make sense of other people's mathematical communication and to make your own more effective.

REPRESENTING MATHEMATICS

Mathematics is abstract in that it is about ideas and relationships, but in order to be communicated these have to be expressed and represented in various ways. Part of learning mathematics is becoming fluent at understanding and using these representations, both for your own use and for communicating with other people (tutors, fellow students, examiners, text authors).

Mathematical communication has three main ingredients: symbols, words and images (see Figure 5.1).

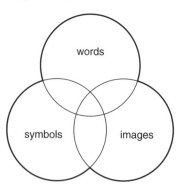

Figure 5.1 Ways of communicating mathematics.

Each of these three contributes to effective understanding and communication, although for any particular topic, purpose or audience one may convey greater meaning than the others. These different ways of communicating mathematics all have their uses, but it is important to be aware of their strengths and limitations. In an important sense, mathematics is a language with a formal grammar, so in mathematical communication involving verbal or symbolic text there are generally accepted conventions (for example, the use of logical connectives like 'and', 'or', 'since' or 'therefore' in correct mathematical sentences), which must be used to ensure successful and accurate communication. The combination of symbols is governed by accepted notational rules.

Task 5.1 Communicating ideas

Think about the following mathematical ideas and techniques and how you might communicate them to others:

1 Pythagoras' theorem.
2 The definition of a rational number.
3 How to solve the equation $2x^2 + x - 28 = 0$.
4 The fact that the angle in a semicircle is always a right angle.

Comment
Idea 1
You may have opted for a purely verbal explanation: 'The square on the hypotenuse is equal to the sum of the squares on the other two sides.'

Or more formally: 'In any planar, right-angled triangle, the square of the length of the hypotenuse is equal to the sum of the squares of the lengths of the other two sides.'

For anyone in the know, this would be sufficient.

For someone not familiar with the theorem, but having a little knowledge of algebra, you might combine a diagram with a formula using symbols (Figure 5.2).

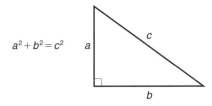

Figure 5.2 A right-angled triangle.

If the questioner had no knowledge of algebra, you might go for:
Area C = Area A + Area B as shown in Figure 5.3.

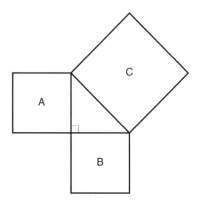

Figure 5.3 Areas A, B and C.

Idea 2

In response to a casual enquiry, you might simply say: 'A rational number is a fraction.'

If asked by a mathematician, you might reply: 'A rational number is a number that can be represented in the form *a* over *b* where *a* and *b* are integers and *b* is not equal to 0.'

You might want to clarify this by writing:

$$\frac{a}{b} \text{ with } a, b \in \mathbb{Z} \text{ and } b \neq 0$$

(The use of such succinct symbolic forms has evolved in the last 500 years, whereas the use of diagrams is over 2000 years old.)

Idea 3

To solve the equation $2x^2 + x - 28 = 0$, you would probably write down something like:

$$(2x \quad)(x \quad) = 0$$

as a first step, or perhaps write out the quadratic formula. In this case, the notation works for you, so a diagram is not the first requirement.

Idea 4

Here a diagram is the key to understanding. Imagine the vertex of the triangle inscribed in the semicircle with the right angle moving around the circle (Figure 5.4).

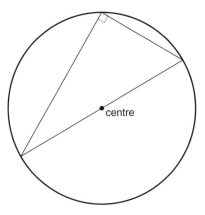

Figure 5.4 Angle in a semicircle.

Once you have drawn this, the meaning would be clear to most people.

The nature of mathematical communication is determined both by the mathematics and by the audience. People can only understand mathematical communications for which they have had the proper preparation. Consider the following statements, which all essentially say the same thing. (Do not worry if you do not recognise any of the three statements, they are just intended to be illustrative.)

- The set of rational numbers is dense in the set of real numbers.
- $\forall r \in \mathbb{R}, \forall \varepsilon > 0, \exists q \in \mathbb{Q}$ such that $|r - q| < \varepsilon$.
- Any real number may be approximated to any level of accuracy by a rational number.

The first is made up of words that, in their everyday sense, would individually be known to most people, but they would be unlikely to be able to understand the meaning of the whole statement. The second is only accessible to someone initiated into the mathematical use of the particular symbols. The third can be understood by anyone who understands the concepts 'real number' and 'rational number' on some level. It is more ambiguous than the first two, because it is not entirely clear if a different rational number is needed for each level of accuracy, or if the same one would do for all levels of accuracy. (What do you think?) To explain this point a diagram, showing part of the real line, might aid the reader's understanding.

When communicating, you have to consider carefully your potential audience and its level of mathematical preparation and preferences, as well as the aim of the communication.

Task 5.2 Your mathematics communication

Who do you think you will need to communicate mathematics to and why?

Comment
Some likely situations are suggested below.

- Communication with fellow students:
  - to check your understanding
  - to help them understand
  - brainstorming to solve problems
  - collaboration in project work
  - revising for examinations
- Communication with lecturers and tutors:
  - to obtain information or clarification
  - for you to check your understanding
  - for them to check your understanding
- Communication with examiners:
  - for you to demonstrate what you know and can do
- Communication with non-mathematicians:
  - to answer questions about everyday mathematics
  - helping non-maths students with mathematical elements of their courses
  - helping friends and relatives with mathematical problems
  - explaining your mathematical studies to friends and family and, perhaps, to potential employers.

READING AND SPEAKING MATHEMATICS

A major part of your studies will involve reading, listening and responding to mathematical language. To be able to make sense of concise written mathematics, you need to be able to 'unpack' it and, to a certain extent, speak it.

Reading about mathematics

Mathematics is written in a highly technical text, using a wide variety of symbols as shorthand forms. There is a variety of linguistic techniques that can be used to help make sense of technical text. Some may seem obvious – others less so – but if you are 'stuck' on interpreting pieces of mathematical writing, it is worth experimenting with the different techniques until you develop a strategy that works for you.

Interpretation

Interpreting a piece of mathematical writing, whether presented as text, diagrams, symbols or a combination of these, means turning it into something that is comprehensible, valid and personally significant. This is much more than merely being able to follow the text. It may involve various combinations of some or all of the following activities:

- reading it out loud
- getting a gist of the overall meaning (perhaps by initially missing out 'difficult' bits)
- making it less dense by unpacking the meanings of individual words and decreasing the volume of symbols by writing them out using words in full
- working on the meanings of technical phrases
- reconstructing and reconstruing the original so that the meaning is clear to you.

Any well-written piece of mathematics is correctly expressed in phrases and sentences. Reading out loud, as if dictating with meaning, rather than simply saying it 'in your head', can help clarify the component sections. It also enables you to hear your own uncertainties; consequently, you can discover the phrases to work on first. It also gives you practice in pronouncing unfamiliar technical terms and in hearing mathematical sentences one after another.

Sections that initially seem incomprehensible may become clearer as you work on the context in which they are used. Where there are key words or symbols that you are not sure of, look them up in a mathematical dictionary. This is not as quick a solution as it may seem, as most dictionary definitions themselves need to be worked on because they may give more or less than you are expecting. If the dictionary does not help you, then you may need to use the Internet (see Chapter 7) or ask someone else. (Ask fellow students, as it will help them to explain to you; if they find it difficult too, then you can all have the confidence to ask your tutor.)

These approaches and techniques are ones you might naturally use when reading more ordinary, hard text (the dense Russian novel, the complex economics article, etc.) and, with practice, you can develop your own strategies for reading mathematics.

Task 5.3 Reading confidently

Find a text from the last mathematics course you took. Read a page or two, as if you were going to have to explain it to someone else.

Think about how you are going to read any symbols – should you read the name of the symbol or its meaning? For example, '+' is often called the plus symbol, but it has two possible meanings: the first, the operation of addition, the other to indicate a positive number. The fraction $\frac{a}{b}$ might be read aloud as 'a over b', 'a divided by b' or 'a b^{ths}' (as in 'four-fifths').

Comment

This activity might have given you an insight into the difference between following a text and reading it with meaning. It is the latter that you need to do when reading for yourself.

Talking about mathematics

There is a big difference between talking in an informal way with fellow students or tutors and making a formal presentation. The main thing in any situation is to have the courage to speak. Most people find this difficult at first; the fear of appearing stupid by not knowing everything or saying something wrong can be very strong. There are several basic ways of overcoming this fear.

- Ease yourself in gently by practising with friends, or even on your own, and in one-to-one situations with tutors. If you are going to see your tutor, look at the material you will be discussing beforehand to give yourself confidence. (This is a good idea anyway, because it will enable you to gain more from the session.)
- Face the fear, and speak up in tutorials even if you are terrified. Just a simple request for clarification, such as 'I don't understand how you get from line 2 to line 3 on the board', will do.
- If you like a more extreme approach, try occasionally admitting ignorance of some basic fact or saying things that you know are somewhat wrong or slightly silly and see what happens. You will find that the sky will not fall on your head – several if not most others will be grateful to you and they may feel encouraged to be more open about their own misunderstandings.

You can help yourself by being well prepared for discussions. This will help you understand and increase your level of involvement in the material and thus increase your enthusiasm and make it easier to communicate. When you are explaining to others, speak clearly – there is no need to rush and be prepared to give extra clarification if necessary. You already understand more mathematics than many of your friends – try to watch out for when you use mathematical jargon that they may find baffling. Remember, they find it as hard to understand you as you do to understand them.

Making a presentation

Although many students perceive this as difficult and stressful, good preparation can go a long way towards alleviating this. The stages of preparation and delivery look something like this.

1 Immerse yourself in the material; get to know it really well. Use a variety of sources, such as lecture notes, books and journals. This is the 'doing mathematics' phase. During this phase, practise talking about the material to anyone who will listen. Note what questions they ask and think of ways of answering them. Keep a file of notes, ideas and diagrams.

2 If the presentation is being marked, find out what the main criteria are and bear them in mind throughout your preparation.

3 Carefully select the material you want to present. Don't try to cram too much into the time available. If you are worried about finishing too early, look for a short, interesting, self-contained item you can use in the last few minutes or omit without loss should you finish the main part on time. Keep your audience in mind: if you are presenting to other students, remember they will have similar difficulties understanding the material as you had yourself, so make sure you give adequate explanation. If you are presenting to examiners, choose material about which you feel confident answering questions. Ask your tutor for advice at this stage.

4 Write out what you want to say. Practise speaking it aloud to get an idea of timing, phrasing and emphasis. You might also want to prepare a reminder sheet for yourself with the main headings and points to remember. You can use this as a prompt sheet on the day.

5 Decide on how you will present text and diagrams. The main possibilities are:
   • black or white board
   • flip chart or prepared poster
   • duplicated handouts
   • overhead projector
   • PowerPoint computer presentation
   • a suitable mathematical computer package (see Chapter 7 for more on using ICT).

6 It is useful to have some visual material prepared beforehand, as this

saves you having to reproduce complicated material on the board. Decide how much technology you want to use: moving computer graphics are fun, but you might find them a distraction if you are nervous on the day. They also take time to prepare, which could be better used for other things. Prepare OHP slides or computer text and images. Do not include too much information on one frame, or plan to change frames too often, as this can be confusing for the audience. Have a flip chart as back-up or be prepared to write on the board if the technology fails.

7 Practise your presentation on friends. Make appropriate changes in the light of this experience.

8 On the day, breathe slowly and deeply, speak clearly, and make eye contact with members of the audience. Do not talk with your back to the audience if writing on the board. Smile!

WRITING MATHEMATICS

To a great extent, mathematics is a written subject. Even if a verbal explanation of something is possible, the listener often cannot hold it in mind unless something is written. For example, if you were to explain that 'A complex number is a number of the form $a + bi$ where a and b are real numbers and i is a square root of -1', the chances are you would want to write down $a + bi$ and $i^2 = -1$ as these are the parts not so easily held in the mind. Part of the purpose of writing mathematics is to stabilise mathematical thoughts, so that they may be more readily understood and revisited.

Sometimes the writing does the work for you, i.e. the conventional notation used is somehow designed to remind you of the steps you need to take. For example, in the calculation:

$$\int_0^\pi \sin x dx = [-\cos x]_0^\pi = -\cos \pi + \cos 0 = 2$$

the notation, once familiar, more or less makes the process automatic.

When writing for other people in a formal way, bear the following points in mind.

1 Before you start writing, make sure you know what you want to say, be clear about the mathematics in your own mind, then, as the March Hare in *Alice in Wonderland* directs, 'say what you mean' and mean what you say.

2 Keep your purpose for writing and your audience in mind. For example, the purpose of an assignment is to show your tutor you know how to solve the problems or construct proofs, so you will want to include some detail of your working, but you can use standard symbols and concepts without explanation. If you are writing for your fellow

students, you will want to include the sorts of reminders that you yourself needed to understand the material originally. If you are writing for the general public, you will have to explain your material without reference to specialist concepts or symbols.

3 Write clearly and in linked sentences. You will need to use mathematical symbols, but when you read your work aloud, including the symbols, it should follow the rules of English grammar and sound like continuous prose. (Note, not all textbooks do this.)

4 Use mathematical symbols correctly. Here are some examples.

- Try not to mix equations with text. For example, write 'c is a constant', rather than 'c = constant'.

- Do not use the '=' sign as a continuity device as in '$2x = 15 = x = 7.5$'. This is obvious nonsense (as it cannot be that $15 = x = 7.5$) and an example of not meaning what you say. Instead, use logical linking words such as 'thus', 'so', 'hence', e.g. $2x = 15$, so $x = 7.5$.

- Use logical symbols such as '⇔' (read as 'if and only if' or 'is equivalent to') and '⇒' (read as 'implies') correctly. Before writing them, consider whether the next line is truly equivalent to or implied by the previous line. If not, use explanatory text, for example:

$$x^3 - 1 = 0$$

$$\Rightarrow (x-1)(x^2 + x + 1) = 0$$

Since x is real, $x = 1$.

Here, the first line and the second are equivalent, so either '⇔' or '⇒' could be correctly used. The equation $x = 1$ does not follow from the second line without the additional explanation, so the symbol '⇒' would not be appropriate.

5 Do not begin assuming what you are trying to prove – this can result in proving that $0 = 0$! This usually arises when checking the solutions to an equation. For example, to show that π is a solution of the equation $\cos\left(\dfrac{3\pi}{2} - x\right) = \sin(x + \pi)$, do not write:

$$\cos\left(\dfrac{3\pi}{2} - \pi\right) = \sin(\pi + \pi)$$

$$\cos\dfrac{\pi}{2} = \sin 2\pi$$

$$0 = 0$$

The fact that '$0 = 0$' follows from the top line but does not logically prove that $x = \pi$ is a solution of the starting equation. Something like the following is preferable.

If $x = \pi$, then

$$\cos\left(\frac{3\pi}{2} - x\right)$$

$$= \cos\frac{\pi}{2}$$

$$= 0$$

Also, $x = \pi$, then

$$\sin(x + \pi)$$

$$= \sin 2\pi$$

$$= 0$$

Hence, $x = \pi$ is a solution of the equation

$$\cos\left(\frac{3\pi}{2} - x\right) = \sin(x + \pi).$$

6 Be careful not to prove the converse of an intended conjecture or theorem.

When writing a longer piece of work, for example writing up a project, the following additional points may be helpful.

1 Keep a folder for 'project ideas' in the weeks before you start writing. At this stage, put in everything that comes to mind.
2 Make an outline plan showing the organisation of the project report into sections and within the sections into discussion, definitions, lemmas, theorems, etc. At this stage, stick to a few main points; do not clutter the report up with secondary material.
3 Discuss the outline with your tutor before starting to write up.
4 Know who your readers will be and judge it accordingly – for instance, just tutors and examiners, or other students as well?
5. Give some thought to the letters of the alphabet you will use to represent mathematical objects. Make sure different objects are assigned different symbols. Careful choice of notation can aid the reader's understanding and poor choice of notation can be very confusing. For example:
   • If you use 'A' to stand for a set, you might use 'a, b, c' to stand for elements of A. However, if you also have a set B you will probably prefer to use a_1, a_2, a_3, ... for the elements of A because '$b \in A$' could be confusing.
   • If you need 'X' to stand for a random variable in section 3, do not have a set called 'X' in section 1.

- If i, j, k are used to stand for unit vectors, do not then use one of the letters i, j, k also as an index, as in $\sum_i^3 = 1^3 a_i b_i$. Use a letter from another part of the alphabet, such as r or s.

To type or not to type?

This is a problem for mathematics students, because mathematical symbols take much longer to type than to write by hand and time spent typing cannot be spent on deep mathematical thought. Obviously some things (projects, dissertations, etc.) may have to be typed, but if you can produce your routine work handwritten (neatly and legibly), this is going to save you time.

Handwriting

Whether you are writing for yourself or someone else you need to write legibly and clearly. It is best to use lots of space, both around and between statements. (This has the added advantage of you being able to add comments where necessary.) Take particular care when writing numbers and symbols – here are some possible ambiguities.

^{superscripts} and $_{\text{subscripts}}$

figure 2, letter zed z

figure 8, Greek delta δ

figure 5, letter ess S, integral symbol $\int$

figure 1, letter el ℓ

figure 9, letter gee g

figure 6, letter bee b

letter x, multiplication symbol $\times$

They may be obvious to you when you write them, but may not be to you (or your tutor) when being read sometime later.

There are also other potential ambiguities that you need to beware of, for example:

$\sqrt{a}b$ means $\sqrt{a} \times b$ not $\sqrt{ab}$

$a + b/c$ means $a + \dfrac{b}{c}$ not $\dfrac{a+b}{c}$. Use of brackets can remove any

chance of ambiguity, e.g.

$a + (b/c)$ or $(a+b)/c$ as appropriate.

Using a word processor

It is the quality of the mathematics that counts. If you do type, there is no need to spend too much time on unimportant typesetting details. But again, subscripts, superscripts and quotients do need particular care. Also the convention is that variables are typed in italics.

Within ordinary word processors, such as MS Word, there are a number of facilities to aid typing mathematics, for example Equation Editor (which creates a graphic). More advanced mathematics typing can be done with programs such as Math Type or Techwriter. But for lengthy advanced work, it may be necessary to learn how to use a specialised mathematical typesetter such as LaTeX. You will be advised, and offered tuition, if this is necessary for your work. (See Chapter 7 for more on using ICT, including hints on using MS Word.) However, for many courses you may only need the very basic facilities offered by MS Word to start with.

DIAGRAMS AND GRAPHS

Diagrams and graphs can play a crucial role in understanding mathematics. When you are communicating mathematics, either verbally or in writing, it makes sense to refer to the graphs and diagrams that you used yourself when working towards understanding the mathematics.

Diagrams

Any diagram should have the following features:

- a title, and possibly a figure number for reference
- clear labelling of aspects that are to be referred to in written work.

If you decide to word process your written work, then it makes sense to use any draw features to produce simple diagrams within the text. For example, MS Word incorporates draw features such as lines and various geometric shapes, as shown in Figure 5.5.

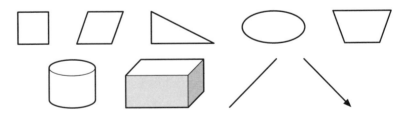

Figure 5.5 Some shapes available in MS Word.

Word also has shapes for producing flow charts, including those shown in Figure 5.6.

Figure 5.6 Some flow-chart shapes available in MS Word.

It is also possible to use more complex drawing packages and import diagrams into the text document. If you have time before your course starts, it may be worth gaining experience with drawing features and packages. However, carefully hand-drawn diagrams are usually acceptable – and often quicker to produce.

Graphs

Graphs are used to provide a visual image of information. This information may be statistical (say, where the graph shows the results of some data collection activity) or may be more abstract (say, showing the behaviour of a mathematical function over a certain range of values). It is important that the reader of the graph can easily extract accurately represented information. There are many graphical images in newspapers, magazines and television news programmes that fail to meet simple standards and consequently are misread or lead to misunderstanding (sometimes intentional).

The best examples of graphs are those that are easy to understand and where the information contained in the graph is easy to find. Producing a good-quality graph takes a little thought and skill. Even when using diagrams and graphs in informal situations, it is important to give your audience enough information to be able to interpret the graph or diagram. Some people are inhibited about asking for clarification and it is a pity if you put effort into drawing something that is not fully appreciated because of lack of information.

Features of a graph
Any graph should have the following features:

- an explanatory title
- labelled axes clearly marked and scaled to show an appropriate range.

Figure 5.7 shows the conventional arrangement for the axes of a graph. Very often, for mathematical graphs such as this, the horizontal axis is labelled 'x' and the vertical axis is labelled 'y'. The place where both 'x' and 'y' values are zero is called the *origin*.

By convention, for statistical graphs the horizontal axis is normally used to display continuous data such as time, length or mass measurements and the vertical axis to display discrete quantities. However, graphs sometimes need to show a relationship between two continuous

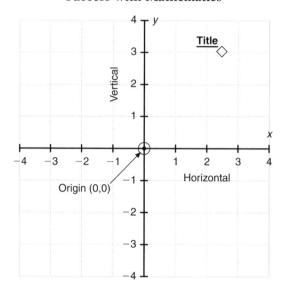

Figure 5.7 Features of a graph.

variables. If one of the variables is time (clock time, days of week, year), then traditionally this should be recorded on the horizontal axis.

The horizontal axis of a graph is normally used for the *independent* variable (chosen) and the vertical axis is used for the *dependent* variable (values that are measured or calculated).

Task 5.4 Independent or dependent?

For each of the following, identify whether the variable is independent or dependent, and whether it matters.

1 Population growth during the last century.
2 Temperature conversion: Fahrenheit/Celsius.
3 Travel graph: distance travelled/time taken.
4 $y = 2x - 3$.

Comment
1 Population growth during the last century – modelling population growth is a time-dependent problem, therefore you should have selected population growth as the dependent variable.
2 Temperature conversion: Fahrenheit/Celsius – in this instance, either variable can be described as the dependent variable; it depends on which way you wish to use the conversion.

3 Travel graph: distance travelled/time taken – because this problem involves time measurements, the distance travelled is the dependent variable.

4 x is the independent variable, because values of y are dependent on the values of x, at least in this presentation of the equation.

Scaling axes appropriately

First, you need to choose a suitable scaling so as to give a clear representation of the data. Care needs to be taken not to exaggerate the scale used, otherwise distortion and misinterpretation of the data can occur.

Second, there are constraints of physical size: for example, the medium being used (paper, overhead projector slide, etc.) and the prominence of the graphical representation.

Third, the scale should be chosen so that individual data points can easily be 'read off' if required.

GRAPHING MATHEMATICAL FUNCTIONS

This section examines:

- plotting coordinates and functions
- graph sketching
- functions.

Plotting coordinates

Cartesian coordinates are used to describe the position of a point within the graphing axis system using the following conventions:

- The horizontal coordinate is quoted first, followed by the vertical coordinate: symbolically, this is written as (x, y).
- The independent variable should be plotted horizontally (on the x-axis) and the dependent variable of a function should be plotted along the vertical scale of the graph (on the y-axis).

Task 5.5 Marking the points

Using an A4 sheet of graph paper with x-axis from -5 to 5 and y-axis scaled from -6 to 6, plot and label the following points:

1 A $(-2, 4)$ 2 B $(2, 5)$ 3 C $(3, -2)$ 4 D $(-3, -3)$

Comment

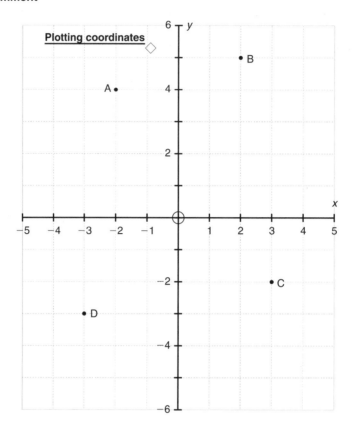

Notice that each axis has been labelled and given a scale: also note that a title has been provided.

For particular purposes, it might be appropriate to write the coordinates of each location adjacent to each letter in the diagram.

Coordinates uniquely identify a particular point within the diagram. This section has only considered two-dimensional planar systems – three-dimensional coordinates appear as (x, y, z).

Plotting functions

To plot a graph of a mathematical function, e.g. $y = 2x + 1$, the use of a *function table* can help to determine sets of coordinates (x, y) that lie on the graph for the function.

x	−4	−3	−2	−1	0	1	2	3	4
2x	−8	−6	−4	−2	0	2	4	6	8
y = 2x+1	−7	−5	−3	−1	1	3	5	7	9

Plotting the pairs of coordinates (x, y) from the top and bottom rows produces the graph shown in Figure 5.8 where the coordinates appear to lie along a straight line.

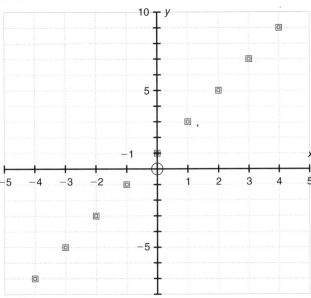

Figure 5.8
Coordinates.

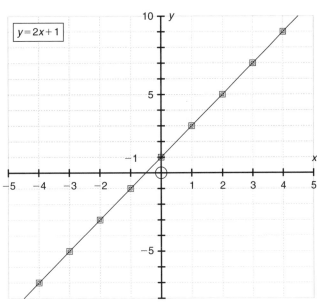

Figure 5.9
y = 2x + 1.

Figure 5.9 shows the graph of the function $y = 2x + 1$.

Notice that in this figure, the line of the graph has been extended beyond the specific points of data. This is called *extrapolation*. Extrapolation suggests that the function being graphed has values that extend beyond the limits being examined. *Interpolation* suggests that the function has values between any two plotted data points.

Sketching functions

There is an important mathematical skill in being able to quickly sketch a graph, as opposed to plotting it accurately. A sketch stresses the important features of the graph, such as its general shape, where it crosses both axes, whether and where it has any peaks or troughs, etc. Such features can be identified using a graph plotter (either calculator- or computer-based), provided the axes are appropriately set. The converse form of this skill is being able to classify different sorts of functions on the basis of their graphs.

If you are asked to sketch a graph, it is generally better to do it by hand if you can. In some cases, where graph-sketching skills are being assessed, you are liable to lose a few marks if you submit a plotted graph, whether plotted by hand or on the computer, rather than a sketch. (You might still get most of the marks if you had correctly labelled everything, marked the axes and the scales and demonstrated your understanding.)

Linear functions

Linear functions (specified by a first-degree equation) can be modelled by the general equation $y = mc + c$ and their graphs are straight lines. The value of m gives the gradient of the line, while c is the y-intercept (in other words, the value of y where the graph crosses the y-axis). The equation is sometimes written as $y = ax + b$ and the reason will become clearer when you look at the parameterised form of the equation specifying a general quadratic function following the next task.

Task 5.6 Sketching linear functions

Sketch (i.e. draw quickly rather than plot accurately) linear functions in the form $y = mx + c$, where:

1 m and c are both positive (e.g. $y = 2x + 1$)
2 m is positive but c is negative (e.g. $y = 2x - 1$)
3 m is negative but c is positive (e.g. $y = -x + 1$)
4 m and c are both negative (e.g. $y = -x - 1$).

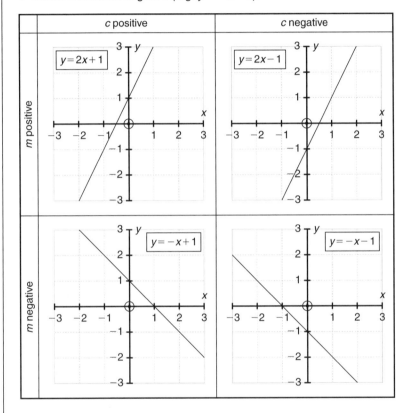

Any linear function can be put in the form $y = mx + c$ by rearranging. For example, $2y = x - 3$ can be rearranged first to:

$$y = \frac{x}{2} - \frac{3}{2}$$

and then to:

$$y = \frac{1}{2}x + \left(-\frac{3}{2}\right), \text{ i.e. } m = \frac{1}{2} \text{ and } c = -\frac{3}{2}.$$

Quadratic functions
Graphs of quadratic functions are parabolas and these functions are specified by the general second-degree equation $y = ax^2 + bx + c$ where $a \neq 0$, as shown in Figures 5.10 and 5.11.

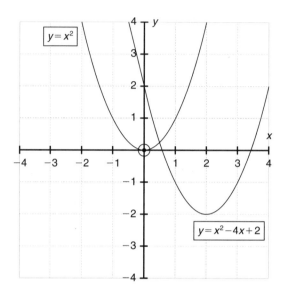

Figure 5.10 When a is positive.

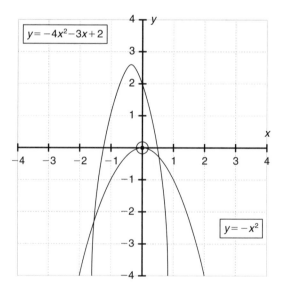

Figure 5.11 When a is negative.

The x-coordinate of the turning point of a quadratic function is $x = -\dfrac{b}{2a}$, and then substituting this value of x into the equation of the function produces the corresponding y-coordinate. Whether and where the graph of a quadratic function intersects the x-axis depends on the solutions, if any, to the quadratic equation $0 = ax^2 + bx + c$ (see Chapter 6 for more on visualising functions).

REFLECTION

Task 5.7 Reflection

Think about the topics and ideas covered in this chapter.

Are there any aspects on which you need to do further work? If so, how are you going to tackle this?

Comment
Perhaps you need to work on the way you write mathematics – for example, your handwriting of symbols may need practice to be more legible and less ambiguous. Or perhaps you are not confident about reading mathematical symbols and need to try speaking mathematics out loud.

You have been reminded that your facility with some aspects of mathematics (algebra, graphs, functions, etc.) may be 'rusty' and that you could need to do some practice.

If anything does need more preparation before you start your course, then you need to plan time to do it.

- Mathematics can be represented in many forms: words, symbols, diagrams and graphs.
- The form(s) used depends on the purpose and the audience.
- The essence of mathematical communication is clarity: being succinct, logical and complete.

6

Learning by doing

This chapter introduces various strategies for working on mathematics, including a section on what it is to understand mathematics. The chapter is for everyone learning mathematics, but may seem challenging to the less confident. If you feel this is you, simply let the ideas wash over you rather than working on them in detail at this stage. You might revisit them at different stages of your course.

INTRODUCTION

Mathematics is not a spectator sport. It is a way of thinking and perceiving, drawing on a sensitivity to certain kinds of opportunities to ask questions and to make sense of the world.

One strategy for studying mathematics is to read as far as you can until you find that you are 'just turning pages'. Much more efficient is to stop and let an idea, a problem, a question work away in the back of your mind while you are walking, washing dishes, sitting on a bus or sleeping. The most important thing you can do to help yourself learn mathematics is to take the initiative. This chapter outlines various actions you can take that will improve your mathematical thinking and help you to take that initiative.

At some point in your studies you are bound to get stuck, to be unable to see what you are supposed to do, or to see what 'it' is about. It will probably even happen in this chapter. There is nothing shameful about this. Indeed, being stuck is an honourable state, for it is only from being stuck and then getting unstuck that you make any real progress in developing your mathematical thinking. By becoming aware of your learnt strategies and natural mental powers, you can enhance your flexibility and facility with mathematical thinking.

In order to get you stuck, and then to help you learn from getting unstuck, this chapter is built around a number of mathematical tasks. These tasks are meant to be worked on immediately you encounter them, not delayed until some later, more convenient time. (This does not mean you have to complete the tasks – think about the best use of your time.) There are no solutions in the back to look up and the comments offered will only make sense if you have seriously thought about the question. So when you encounter a task, read it, close the book and reconstruct it in your mind – then work on it. Return to the book only when you have been able to say something to someone else about the problem (in the absence of a willing listener, write notes to yourself, or talk to an imaginary friend). Tell them either why you are stuck (what you find you cannot do but want to be able to do) and what you have tried to do about being stuck, or what you did that was successful. When you do read the comments, if you suddenly get an idea, then stop reading and go back and work out its implications before reading further. This does require discipline, but it is a discipline well worth developing.

The advice in this chapter is based on three ideas.

1 We all have enormous powers to think mathematically when we are born. It is up to us to develop and make use of these powers (even when previous bad experiences may have reduced our confidence).
2 There are some major themes that both drive and interconnect across mathematics and having these come to mind can help make sense of a topic when you are in the thick of studying it.
3 Treating mathematics as a constructive activity supports and underlines the need to be active with respect to mathematical ideas, to worry at them the way a dog will worry at a bone, to take initiative in a constructive manner. Taking this sort of a stance equips you to make progress, as well as preparing you to ask probing and useful questions of a tutor or fellow student.

MENTAL POWERS

This section draws attention to some fundamental powers for making sense of the world and which are particularly useful in mathematical thinking.

Imagining and expressing

Task 6.1 The tethered goat

Consider the following question:

> A goat has been tethered with a 6 m line to an outside corner of a 4 m by 5 m rectangular shed. What area of grass can the goat reach?

Do not put pen to paper until you have formed an image in your mind. (You are not being asked to solve this problem here.)

Comment

If you felt a strong desire to draw a diagram, then good. What was the force that made you want to draw? Did you have a mental image? Some people have mental pictures, but want to capture them, hold them still, because they tend to be either fleeting or unstable. Other people work better with words; they sometimes need encouragement to 'draw a diagram'. But it is important to note that the work takes place on your 'mental screen', not on the page. The page is good for stabilising images. The diagram is an expression of your image, whether that image is verbal, pictorial, visceral or some combination of all of these.

What is certain is that the power to imagine can be strengthened and one way to do this is to pause before drawing a diagram and trying to imagine as much as you can before expressing it on paper.

If you have not already drawn a diagram, then do so now. It does not have to be accurate or measured, but it needs to capture the essence of the situation. For example, the shed is rectangular, not square, and the tether is longer than either side of the shed. Include on your diagram the extreme positions the goat can reach.

Now use your diagram to form an image of where the goat can reach as it moves from one extreme point to another.

There is a curious symbiotic relationship between the mental world and the world of the diagram. It is sometimes as if you are looking through the specifics of the diagram and seeing intermediate states and positions, a bit like looking at holiday or family photos and using them to recall and reconstruct events that took place around the same time or in the same place. Here, you can almost feel the goat tugging at the tether, as it sweeps around from one position to another. As it moves, it is constrained by the other end of the tether, either at the tether point or additionally on the corner of the building.

The region the goat can reach is thus made up of a collection of portions of circles, so the actual area can be calculated.

What can be learned from the tethered goat problem so far?

The desire to draw a diagram in response to a mathematical problem is an important one. It involves a process of stabilising thoughts, which tend to be fleeting and ephemeral in nature. Symbols and diagrams help to pin down some elements or aspects, in order to enable you to enter the world of the problem mentally and sort out what you know (from the givens in the problem and from what you know generally) that seems relevant to what you want. The two questions:

• What do I know?
• What do I want?

are very, very helpful. Jotting down answers to them rarely takes more than a few seconds and can serve to stabilise your thinking, in order that you can concentrate on the important parts.

Expressing your images by writing down thoughts and possibilities can also afford access to them later, for despite the belief that 'it seems obvious so I won't forget it', ideas and conjectures slide in and out of awareness terribly quickly. Furthermore, if, as is likely to happen when you are studying, you find you have to put your work aside and attend to something else, it can be very difficult to pick up again from where you were unless you have a record of what you were thinking. So recording answers to:

- What do I know?
- What do I want?

and jotting down things like:

- I wonder if …?
- Maybe …?

can actually help to clarify your thinking now, as well as affording access to it again later. Here is another task on which to test some of the assertions made so far.

Task 6.2 Quadratic chords

(This is a more challenging task, more suitable for those who found the tethered goat problem easy to visualise.)

Imagine the graph of $y = x^2$. Now imagine two points on the graph. Allow those two points to move anywhere they like, as long as they stay on the graph.

When you are comfortable with that image, imagine the chord drawn between the two points and mark the mid-point of the chord. Again, allow the end points of that chord to move anywhere they like, as long as they stay on the graph.

Where can the mid-point of the chord get to?

Reminder: do not draw a diagram until you really feel you have to.

Comment

With practice, you can become quite good at allowing objects to move in your mind and get a sense of where they can go (invoking the general ideas of freedom and constraint). A sensible thing to do is to *specialise* by making things simpler. For example, hold one end of the chord fixed and only allow the other end to move. Where can the mid-point get to under this extra restriction (a special case of the question asked)?

A diagram might help you see that this involves a scaling process, because the moving end of the chord produces a mid-point that each time is halfway to the fixed point along the chord. So the result must be a scaled parabola. Then allowing the fixed end to move as well produces a family of scaled parabolas that fill the inside space formed by the original parabola.

Specialising and generalising

Task 6.3 Remaindered

Write down a number that leaves a remainder of 1 on being divided by 5.
    How many such numbers can you find between 1 and 50?
    Now write down another such number that is also larger than a million.
    Describe in words, if not in symbols, how to construct all numbers that leave a remainder of 1 on being divided by 5.
    Generalise, characterising all those numbers that leave a remainder of r on being divided by d.

Comment
The first part of the task is quite particular. The second part is trying to prompt your awareness of a range of choices and of the necessary structure of those choices. This is enhanced by the third part, which requires some awareness that it is all numbers of the form of 1 plus some multiple of 5. The fourth part explicitly asks for description of structure and the fifth part explicitly invites your generalising of both the remainder and the divisor.

The move from particular to general, from focusing on a particular (say, *remainder* and *divisor*) to seeing through these particulars to a generality is perhaps the most basic of mathematical moves. It is something you have done many times in getting to grips with learning language, but it is something that requires explicit attention in mathematics. You need to be able to move from $1 + 5n$ as an expression representing the construction of all numbers with a remainder of 1 on being divided by 5 to seeing that the 1 is a place-holder for the remainder and the 5 is a place-holder for the divisor. So, in general (a common mathematical expression), $r + dn$ represents all possible numbers leaving a remainder of r on being divided by d, where n is permitted to be any integer whatsoever.

Task 6.4 Consecutive products

Which numbers can be formed by adding 1 to the product of four consecutive (whole) numbers?

Comment
Your immediate response was almost certainly to try an example. This is the basic meaning of the word *specialising*: looking for a particular or special case related to the question to try things out on. The purpose at first is to get a sense of what the generality is saying or, in this case, what the question is suggesting. It may take several examples before you begin to detect a pattern, which in this instance depends on recognition of the sorts of numbers you get as answers. Sometimes, it is useful to specialise almost randomly (e.g. try $10 \times 11 \times 12 \times 13 + 1$), but more often than not it helps to specialise systematically.

$$1 \times 2 \times 3 \times 4 + 1 = 25 \qquad 3 \times 4 \times 5 \times 6 + 1 = 361$$

$$2 \times 3 \times 4 \times 5 + 1 = 121 \qquad 4 \times 5 \times 6 \times 7 + 1 = 841$$

The first two examples are readily recognisable as 5^2 and 11^2, which might suggest checking to see if the others are also squares. They turn out to be 19^2 and 29^2 respectively. So it looks as if we might be getting square numbers, and odd squares at that. But this is, at best, a tentative conjecture, something that *might* be true. Can you predict what the numerical answer will be in terms of the four consecutive numbers you started with?

Look for a relationship between the square root of the answer and the four consecutive numbers used. Test out any conjectures on a few more examples. Would it help to consider the consecutive numbers 0, 1, 2, 3 or $-1, 0, 1, 2$?

As mentioned previously, specialising is an entirely natural and very useful strategy for getting a sense of generality about what is being asked or asserted. When a learner asks for help on a problem, the question 'Can you specialise in some way?' is usually the first question asked and very often leads to immediate progress. But the main force of specialising is to assist in the reverse process, namely *generalising*. You try out special or particular cases, not just to get some examples to stare at, but also in order to get a sense of what is going on. In this case, it required a flash of insight to see how the square root of the answer can be predicted from the four particular consecutive numbers that gave rise to that answer. Some sort of access to the structure of the situation as a whole is required.

One approach is to look at partial products: do you simply multiply the four consecutive numbers in order, or do you look for an easier way? What happens if you multiply the outside pair and the inside pair separately *before* then multiplying them altogether? Another approach is to use algebra, which can be a good way of detecting and expressing structure.

Algebra is the primary language of expressing generality in mathematics. It is effective, because it is both an expressive language and one whose expressions can readily be manipulated.

Task 6.5 Structuring

Express the structure of Task 6.4 using four consecutive numbers starting with *n*.

Multiply the outside two and the inside two numbers separately, before multiplying the results together and then finally adding 1 to get the full result.

Comment

For people already confident with symbols, using an *n* is actually a form of specialising, for specialising means 'turning to some confidently manipulable entities' as a particular or special case. This might mean using physical objects, numbers, symbols for general or arbitrary numbers, functions, and so on.

Before you multiply the expression out and seek to factor it as a perfect square (do you have a conjecture yet as to *which* square it is as an expression involving *n*?), you might want to consider whether starting with $n-1$ rather than *n* might make the calculations easier. It is always worthwhile pausing before implementing a strategy or computation to ask yourself if there might be another, better way.

Specialising is a natural response to generality. Its main role, once the generality is understood, is to assist in re-expressing the general through locating underlying structure. It is worth paying attention to how you do the particular calculations or drawings as much as to the result obtained. For example, in Task 6.2, fixing one end of the chord and allowing just the other end to move reveals an entirely new dimension to the situation, the notion of scaled copies of the original curve. Notice that this applies more generally to any starting curve, not just to the particular parabola $y = x^2$. So specialising does indeed assist generalising.

> • Specialising and generalising lie at the heart of mathematical thinking. But they also lead to useful study techniques. Each mathematical technique that you encounter, as well as each theorem or mathematical fact, is itself a generality.

In order to appreciate that generality, it is useful to become aware of the range and scope of the generality: what is permitted to change and what *has* to stay the same? Before looking at some mathematical topics, think back to the Tethered goat problem (Task 6.1).

Task 6.6 The tethered goat revisited

What features of the original problem could be changed without altering the basic problem?

Comment
There are three specific numbers in the original problem. Any or all of these could be altered. Of course, if the tether is too long, the goat might wind itself around the shed a few times, so that might make a slight difference to the calculation of the area, but the basic approach would remain the same: break the region into portions of a circle and then add them together.

What other details are specified in the task? For example, the shed is rectangular. Could that be changed and still the approach remain much the same? What if it were a triangle, or a quadrilateral, or a pentagon, or ...? What if it were a circular shed?

The goat is tethered to a corner. Does it matter *which* corner? What if it were tethered somewhere part-way along one edge – would that make much difference to the area it can reach?

Suddenly, it is not clear whether the same technique would work or whether we might need some more powerful mathematics.

What if the goat were tethered not to a single point, but to a ring that could slide along a wire pegged at each end to the ground, perhaps with one end at a corner of the shed?

And now that we are really extending things, what if the goat were tethered in space? Physically, it is silly – goats can jump but cannot fly – but *mathematically* there might be some interest. Does the technique change appreciably if we seek the volume of space accessible to a goat on a tether of given length at the corner of, say, a cuboid of given dimensions?

There are rather too many questions here! But the process is important. In order to get a sense of the original question, it is important to see what aspects can be varied and how. That way, you can acquaint yourself with possibilities so that in the future you are more likely to recognise a variant of something you have already done. A useful way of thinking about this is to ask yourself the following questions.

- What can or might be changed?
- What is the range or scope of variation?
- In what ways can a given aspect be changed?

Exactly the same questions are useful whenever you encounter a collection of exercises or problems illustrating a technique. Ask yourself what can change, and in what way, without significantly affecting how the technique is used.

Conjecturing and convincing

Arithmetic is about calculating answers using the four operations on numbers. Mathematics is also about getting answers, but often those answers are rather more difficult to find and do not consist simply of a single number. Mathematics is much more about making *conjectures*: that is, expressing in words, diagrams and symbols generalities that you think might hold. It also involves testing those conjectures against more examples, trying to see what might be going on and under what conditions the conjecture holds. Ultimately, you want to be able to justify your conjecture to others. The aim of mathematics is to convince others that a conjecture in fact *always* (or sometimes that it *never*) holds under stated conditions.

Returning to Task 6.4, particular cases certainly suggest that the answers are always squares of odd numbers. You can convince yourself that at least it must always be *odd*, because you are adding one to the product of four consecutive numbers, some two of which *must* be even (why is that?), so that the overall answer has to be odd. The process of convincing, of justifying your conjectures, can be a long process. Proofs do not spring straight from the pens of even experienced mathematicians. They too can struggle, sometimes for months or years, to express succinctly but clearly what they see, feel and have come to know from their experience. You start by trying to convince yourself. Then you try your idea, claim or proof on interested friends. When you find yourself augmenting what you say or write, you modify your exposition, the aim being to be able to convince someone who is sceptical but not present, so that you cannot keep adding in extra details. This is done by putting forward reasons for assertions that you make that build up to agreement that your conjecture is indeed valid.

(The word *theorem*, which is so important to mathematicians, actually comes from the ancient Greek word *theorein* meaning *a seeing*. To develop a proof therefore means, at heart, to arrange that others can see what you see in the way you see it.)

Organising and characterising

Even young children have the power and the desire to classify and organise, which in mathematics leads to categorising. For example, in the case of Task 6.4, the conjecture that the answer is always an odd square is a start, but clearly you cannot get *all* odd squares this way, so there is more work to be done to classify precisely *which* odd squares can actually appear in the list of numbers generated in this way. Working out exactly which odd numbers can be the square root of the answer is a process of characterising. In this case, it turns out to be all and only those numbers that can be written in the form $n^2 + 3n + 1$, for these are the square roots of the product of the four consecutive numbers starting with n. Perhaps more usefully, they can also be expressed as $(n + 1)(n + 2) - 1$ (one less than the product of the middle two numbers of the four you started with): in other words, as 'one less than the product of two consecutive numbers'. The careful mathematical thinker pauses and asks:

- Are all numbers that are one *more* than the product of four consecutive numbers themselves one *less* than the product of two consecutive numbers?
- Are all numbers that are one *less* than the product of two consecutive numbers the square root of one *more* than the product of four consecutive numbers?

If the answer is yes to both questions, then the answer has been characterised, for it is known not only that they all have a certain form, but that all numbers of that form do actually arise in this way. Thus:

> A number is one more than the product of four consecutive numbers *if and only if* it is the square of a number that is one less than the product of two consecutive numbers. (Mathematicians often write such characterising claims using the phrase *if and only if*, usually shortened to *iff*. The mathematical symbol for this phrase is ⟺, as was mentioned in the previous chapter.)

This process illustrates what specialising means in its broadest terms – always replace what is fuzzy with something relevant and more particular that is more confidence-inspiring, whatever that may be. But remember: the main purpose of specialising is to get a sense of the general. In order to cope with increasing complexity, you need to appreciate and gain experience with generalities, which you do first by specialising, and then by using that specialisation to reconstruct the generality for yourself. In this way, you prepare yourself to be able to reconstruct the ideas and their relation to one another again when you need them and not be dependent on rote memorisation.

Twentieth-century mathematics made great leaps forward through the process of building on the notion of characterising objects by their properties. For example, the expression $2n + 1$ expresses the fact that no matter which whole number you substitute for n, the answer will always be odd. Furthermore, *any* odd number can be so expressed. So the algebraic expression $2n + 1$ *characterises* odd numbers.

Task 6.7 Classifying parallelograms

Show that in any parallelogram, the diagonals always bisect each other.

Further, show that if the diagonals of a quadrilateral bisect each other, then the quadrilateral must be a parallelogram.

Comment
How could you 'show that'? Recall that 'show' was one of those words discussed in Chapter 4 (Working on individual questions), where it was described as signalling 'justify each step and produce a convincing argument'. So, you have to find some justification that is independent of any particular parallelogram: therefore, the task is finding an argument that draws on some property that applies to them all. But to do this it helps to draw a particular parallelogram. In drawing one, ask yourself if there are any extreme cases or variations: for example, a very long and thin one, as well as the more usual nearly-rhombic parallelogram:

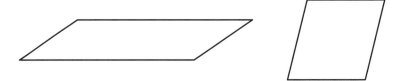

What facts can be assembled? What is *known* for sure? The figure is a parallelogram, which means that pairs of opposite sides are both equal in length and parallel. What is *required* is to see why this means that the diagonals *must* bisect each other. So one obvious thing to do is to draw in those diagonals:

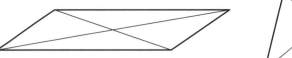

Take two of the little internal triangles that are opposite each other. Because they come from a parallelogram, the edges opposite the common vertex are equal and parallel, so the angles formed there are correspondingly equal. So the two triangles are congruent and consequently all corresponding pairs of sides are equal, which forces the common vertex to be the mid-point of both diagonals.

Notice that paying attention to what was known, and juxtaposing that with what is wanted, leads to distinguishing certain details or features and then using these to connect to what was wanted. Also, it helped to focus attention on only part of the diagram.

For the second part of the task, we are told that the diagonals of a quadrilateral bisect each other, and we want to see why the quadrilateral *has* to be a parallelogram. What do we know now? We *know* that the diagonals bisect one another. What we *want* is to discover why the quadrilateral must therefore be of a particular type, namely a parallelogram.

One way to see this is to focus on the mid-point where the diagonals cross and to consider the two triangles formed by just one of the diagonals. The two triangles must be congruent, because each is formed by reflecting each of its vertices in the mid-point of the diagonal (using the fact that the diagonals bisect). Once the triangles are congruent, the equality and the parallelism of opposite sides follows from the angle properties of parallel lines and a transversal (a line crossing them).

Parallelograms can therefore be classified or characterised by a property of their diagonals. If the diagonals bisect, the quadrilateral is a parallelogram; if the quadrilateral is a parallelogram, the diagonals bisect. Identification of a property, and then showing that that property characterises objects, is one of the principal activities of mathematics.

Notice that, when you are unsure or stuck, a powerful device is to ask yourself

- What do I know? (it rarely takes long to write it all down)
- What do I want? (it is awfully easy to lose track of this)
- Can I construct a simple or simpler example? (in order to try to see what is going on in general).

Task 6.8 Classifying quadratics

The graph of any quadratic equation (one of the form $y = ax^2 + bx + c$) can be transformed into $y = x^2$ by translating and scaling. Thus, there is really only one kind of quadratic (to within equivalence by translation and scaling).

Think of a quadratic graph without any axes. What this assertion is claiming is that you can choose the axes so as to make the equation of the graph, relative to these new axes, be $y = x^2$. How might this be done?

Comment

The graph of $y = x^2$ has the origin at the lowest point of the graph, and the y-axis as the line of symmetry, so put the axes in that position. This is effectively translating the curve to the axes (or the axes to the curve). Scaling the y-axis relative to the x-axis enables the coordinates to be matched by those generated by $y = x^2$.

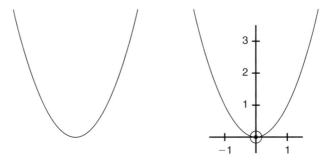

Algebraically, what has happened is that the original equation has been rewritten.

$$y = ax^2 + bx + c$$

This is the same equation as:

$$y = a\left(x^2 + \frac{bx}{a}\right) + c. \quad \text{(Can you see why?)}$$

This is still the same as:

$$y = a\left[x^2 + \frac{b}{a}x + \left(\frac{b^2}{4a^2}\right)\right] + c - \left(\frac{b^2}{4a}\right)$$

(because adding and subtracting the same amount, $\dfrac{b^2}{4a}$, makes no difference to the fact of equality).

This can be rewritten as:

$$y = a\left(x + \frac{b}{2a}\right)^2 + c' \text{ (using } c' = c - \frac{b^2}{4a}, \text{ which is another constant)}$$

$$y - c' = a\left(x + \frac{b}{2a}\right)^2$$

This is in the form of a translation (subtract c' from the y-coordinate and add $\frac{b}{2a}$ to the x-coordinate) and then a scaling of the y-axis relative to the x-axis (by the numerical factor a). So this is the specification of how to choose those new axes, relative to which this equation will be $y = x^2$.

Notice that this also shows algebraically how a quadratic equation can be translated and scaled so that its graph can be made to match that of $y = x^2$. To characterise fully all quadratic equations as being 'similar', it still needs to be explained that algebraically a general quadratic has been used, whereas geometrically it was assumed that the starting quadratic was the 'right' way up. If it had been the other way up, we would have had to flip it over (which is signalled by the first parameter a being negative), which then forms part of the necessary scaling.

Task 6.9 Classifying cubics

Try something similar with a general cubic equation $y = ax^3 + bx^2 + cx + d$.

Claim: There are only three 'essentially different' kinds of cubic equations (to within equivalence by means of translation and scaling).

Comment

Geometrically, the axes can be placed wherever, but no amount of scaling will alter the basic wiggles in the graph of a cubic that comes in these three different types:

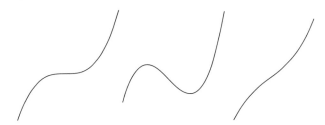

The question is whether these are what characterise graphs of cubic equations.

Looking back over the algebra for the quadratic equation, the strategy was as follows: remove the scale factor a from the leading coefficient by factoring it out; express the terms involving x as perfect squares; sort out the new constant. Perhaps something similar will work here? Notice how using 'what is the same and what is different' is turning a result into a strategy.

$$y = ax^3 + bx^2 + cx + d$$

$$y = a\left(x^3 + \frac{b}{a}x^2 + \frac{c}{a}x\right) + d$$

$$y = a\left(x + \frac{b}{3a}\right)^3 + cx - \frac{b^2}{3a}x + \left(d - \frac{b^3}{27a^2}\right)$$

$$y = a\left(x + \frac{b}{3a}\right)^3 + \left(c - \frac{b^2}{3a}\right)x + \left(d - \frac{b^3}{27a^2}\right)$$

If the coefficient of the additional x-term $\left(\text{namely } c - \dfrac{b^2}{3a}\right)$ is zero, you get the cubic $y = x^3$, which is the first graph depicted above. If the coefficient of that extra x-term is negative, the x-axis and the y-axis can be scaled so as to get the cubic $y = x(x^2 - 1)$, the second one in the above diagram. If the coefficient of this term is positive, the x-axis and the y-axis can be scaled so as to get the cubic $y = x(x^2 + 1)$, the third graph shown above.

The fine details are not important here. What matters is you experiencing the process of characterising, of showing that if you stress shape and ignore position (translation) and permit scaling (stretching or shrinking one axis scale relative to the other), then there is effectively only one quadratic and only three types of cubics. This latter result was achieved by generalising the argument strategy for quadratics.

MATHEMATICAL THEMES

Mathematics sometimes comes across to novices as a huge collection of definitions, ideas, facts and techniques. But to the more experienced, mathematics reflects a rich web of interconnections. Problems that appear to belong to one kind of thinking can suddenly be resolved by seeing them as belonging to an entirely different kind of thinking. One of the ways in which to see and experience links between apparently disparate mathematical topics is to become aware of dominant themes that run through mathematics. Here are four that have emerged in the work you have done so far.

Doing and undoing

Whenever you can get an answer to a problem (for example, by using a technique), you can turn things around and ask yourself: 'If someone provides the answer, is it possible to work out what the particular question was?'

For example, you can add one to the product of four consecutive numbers. That is a 'doing', a calculation. But if someone gives you a number, can you work out whether it came from such a calculation (and if so, which one)? That was the essence of Task 6.4. You could use the same idea to reverse the tethered goat problem (Task 6.1): if someone gave you an area, what shapes of shed and lengths of tether would produce that area? You could even specify the shape of the shed in advance and simply ask whether there is a tether (a length and a place to attach it) that would produce that area, or vice versa, specify the tether length and location and then seek feasible shed dimensions. Classifying or characterising, as with the quadrilaterals and the graphs, is essentially a doing and undoing process, for having identified a property (doing), you ask whether that property is sufficient to characterise the objects (undoing).

Invariance amidst change

Many mathematical facts or results can be seen as specifying something (usually a property or relationship) that is invariant amidst various features changing. For example, 'the sum of the angles of a planar triangle is 180 degrees' states an invariant (the sum of the angles) but downplays what is allowed to change (the shape of the triangle). This invariance can be slightly emphasised by changing '… of a planar triangle' to '… of *any* planar triangle' or by changing '… is 180 degrees' to '… is *always* 180 degrees'. The property of having 'diagonals bisecting each other' is invariant among *all* parallelograms, as well as characterising parallelograms among *all* quadrilaterals, so there are effectively two invariants here (the bisecting property and that of being a parallelogram). The property of being the square of an odd number is an invariant among *all* numbers of the form 'one more than the product of four consecutive numbers'. The shape of a number that leaves a remainder of 1 on being divided by 3 is invariant, namely $3n + 1$.

Whenever you encounter a technique, it is worth asking yourself what the dimensions of variation might be (what can change and yet still the technique can be used) and what the range of change is in each case.

Extending and contracting meaning

When children first encounter number, it means a counting number. Later, the meaning and use of the term is extended to negatives, fractions, decimals, and perhaps more. Thus, in mathematics, the meaning of a term is often extended because the new objects are similar to the old ones in the properties that they satisfy. But, in mathematics, meaning can also sometimes be contracted. For example, the term 'fraction' is not used to mean simply 'a part of', as in, 'I only ate a fraction of the cake'. Familiar words are sometimes used with a more restricted meaning and it is important to recognise when this is happening.

Freedom and constraint

Much of mathematics can be seen as concerning some object (perhaps a number, or a shape, or some other object), which begins as being totally free. It can be *any* value, *any* shape, *any* object. But then constraints are imposed, usually in the form of properties or relationships that are often manifested as equations or inequalities. The task is then to decide if there is any such object possible that actually meets all those constraints. Sometimes there are no such objects, sometimes a unique one and sometimes many. In this way, many mathematical tasks can be seen as construction tasks and mathematics can be seen as a constructive activity, one which often involves enormous creativity, a far cry from being dominated by memorisation and application of well tried and tested techniques.

> • Mathematics is a constructive activity: every technique, every theorem, every definition provides an opportunity to engage in creative construction.

LEARNING BY COMMUNICATING

If you recall that the word 'theorem' has as its root meaning 'to look' or 'seeing', then understanding mathematics is about learning to 'see' in the sense of 'I see what you are saying', and communicating mathematics is about acting so that others too can see what you are seeing. The question, then, is whether you are clearly 'saying what you see, so that others can see what you are saying'.

In the previous sections, it was suggested that writing down conjectures was useful, if only to provide something to return to when you get lost or after a period of letting the problem mull a bit in the back of your mind. Although it is perfectly possible to go off into your own world of mathematics, as soon as you want to share your excitement at some insight, you have to communicate to someone else. But, in fact, other people can also be very useful as foils for clarifying ideas for yourself.

There is an old adage that the best way to learn something thoroughly is to teach it. This can be exploited by using anyone who will listen, and if no humans are available, then an actual or virtual goldfish or other pet can serve almost as well.

> • Find someone or something to act as audience.
>
> (They do not have to understand what you are saying, writing or drawing, though of course it helps if they try.)

Here are some tasks to try through which you can encounter most of the points being made in the rest of this chapter and which will be used to illustrate those points.

Task 6.10 Tangential

Through which points in the plane is it possible to find a line tangent to the curve $y = x^2$?

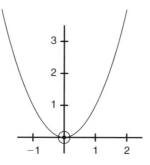

And what about the curve $y = x(x - 1)(x + 1)$?

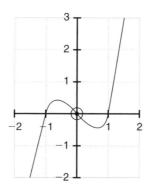

Convince yourself and then a friend.

Comment

You may find it useful to draw your own picture; to use a pencil or piece of paper as a straight-edge; to formulate a conjecture; to try to articulate that conjecture in words. You may find that the algebra is straightforward, but if so, try the same problem on a quartic (a graph arising from a fourth-degree equation) or on the graph of $y = \tan x$.

What is special about these two curves? Can you express a general 'algorithm' for finding those points of tangency?

What is different about convincing yourself from convincing a friend?

Task 6.11 One sum

Take two numbers that sum to 1. Calculate two new numbers as follows: square the larger and add the smaller; square the smaller and add the larger. Which of your two answers do you think will be the bigger?

Formulate a conjecture; test it; convince yourself and then a friend that your conjecture is *always* true.

Comment

Almost certainly you tried some specific numbers first. Perhaps you were surprised by the results. But will the same thing always happen?

You may feel convinced after trying a few examples. But this is still only suggestive, not convincing. To be fully convinced, you have to be able to demonstrate that no matter which pair of numbers (subject to the constraint that they sum to 1, of course), the same thing will always happen.

The only way to do this for all possible such pairs is to use algebra to express the generality. It begins with something like:

> Let x be one of the numbers. Then ... is the other number. Then the square of one plus the other is ..., etc.

UNDERSTANDING MATHEMATICS

What does it mean to say 'I understand numbers' or 'I understand functions'? On one level, if you can do the questions you are set, especially the assessment tasks, then presumably you can claim that you understand. But very often it is possible to do set tasks using other worked examples as a template. At the end, have you really understood? One approach is to ask yourself: Could I do a problem like this again?

It is one thing to 'get a solution' and quite another to appreciate how it was achieved and to feel confident that you could do it again in the future. There is a very important feature to this question, for it asks about 'a problem *like this*'. One of the most useful things you can do when studying mathematics, whether reading through a worked example, doing an exercise or responding to a task, is to try to work out what makes a problem or example be 'like this' or 'of this type'. In other words, try to generalise the problem or task, in the ways suggested in this chapter, by considering:

- What could change (what are the dimensions of variation) and yet this would still be a question 'of the same type': that is, one which would succumb to the same strategies?

- What is the range of change that is possible within those dimensions of variation?

In an ideal world, you could try to express in your own words what you think the most general problem or task of this type is and ask your tutor to confirm that this does indeed capture the full range of variation and change.

Understanding has many aspects. Some people feel they understand when they can talk aloud about the process involved in solving a problem; others like to have a clear 'picture' or sense of what the problem is about and how the technique works; others still like to have everything distilled down to a few symbols. It is worth becoming aware of your preferences; it is also well worthwhile strengthening those dimensions in which you are less confident. For example, trying to strengthen your mental imagery is a valuable component of thinking, as is trying to gain facility in using symbols to express your thoughts – as is also learning to give verbal instructions to someone as to how to use a technique, rather than simply 'showing them' or 'doing it for them'.

> - Find out your preferences. Strengthen ways of expressing yourself with which you are less confident.

EXPRESSING YOURSELF MATHEMATICALLY

Although symbols are most often associated with doing and communicating mathematics, words and pictures also play an important role.

Convincing as a process

Most mathematics is encountered as words and symbols with the occasional diagram. But those words and symbols, those diagrams, have not simply popped out of someone's head. It can take many, many drafts before a mathematician is satisfied that the logic and the argument are presented as clearly as possible and yet without unnecessary extras that get in the way. So when you are trying to communicate your understanding to someone else, you cannot expect it to be perfectly clear first time.

What tends to happen is that you become convinced that something is the case or that you can see how to get an answer to justify a conclusion. Then you try to express it to yourself. Sometimes, it helps just to say it out loud: this can help some people to clarify, to expose gaps or uncertainties. Sometimes a diagram or a sequence of diagrams can help. Once the articulation begins to flow, try writing it down. Then it is best to leave it for a little, before reading over critically. This means catching yourself when a rich mental image or memory of being convinced comes to mind and trying to act like someone who is reading what you have written for the first time. If you have included comments such as:

I know ... and I want ...,

then you will probably find it much easier to make sense of your notes and of your articulation. A tutor or exam marker will also find it much easier to read. At some stage, as you gain confidence, it helps to show it to a friend who, precisely because of *not* having your past experience of thinking about the problem, is more likely to look at the explanation freshly. Thus, they are more likely to identify gaps or blunders or simply places that lack clarity. It is ideal if you can find a willing fellow student, so that you can play this role for each other, but the aim eventually is for you to be able to play that role for yourself. You are looking for places where they ask for clarification, or where they get stuck. Then you can augment your explanation or otherwise adjust it, because ultimately you want something that will stand alone without you there to 'back it up' or to 'fill in details' or to 'explain what was meant' when the reader gets stuck.

All of this can be summarised as three phases or types of convincing:

- convincing yourself
- convincing a friend
- convincing a distant sceptic.

These phases describe a back-and-forth movement, not a fixed, one-way progression. Even experts find themselves questioning what they thought they knew, so these three phases can be seen as descriptive of the development of assignments to hand in to a tutor; of the development of an explanation of some insight that you have had; of the development of understanding over the longer term. Every opportunity to explain to someone else is valuable, helping you come to fresh insights and appreciate more connections.

A mathematical proof is a convincing, complete, succinct and logical argument that demonstrates a particular truth.

- Expect to make several drafts as you first try to convince yourself, then use a friend or colleague (or goldfish) to refine your descriptions and expressions, before gradually developing a version that might stand on its own.

- Try to justify each step of your explanation, if only by referring to a stated theorem or a technique from a previous section or chapter.

- Do not hide your uncertainties; ask your tutor for assistance in providing reasons; do not be afraid to do what you can and then to ask for help as to the next step. Make and acknowledge conjectures where you cannot see how to justify assertions you want to make; include comments such as 'I want ...', 'I know ...' and 'If only I could ..., then I would be able to ...'.

REFLECTION

This chapter has introduced various strategies for working on mathematics and was built around a number of tasks, some of which you may well have found quite challenging.

Task 6.12 On being stuck

Think back to a task on which you became 'stuck' and then managed to become 'unstuck'. Think about what happened. How did you resolve the problem? List a number of strategies that you might employ when you become 'stuck'.

Comment

Being 'stuck' is an honourable state and there are a number of strategies that can make this a positive experience rather than simply a negative feeling.

- Acknowledge that you are stuck – relax and recognise that this is a learning opportunity. Different people develop different strategies for dealing with being stuck. Whatever you do, do not panic.
- Next, try to identify exactly *why* you are stuck. This process is, in effect, identifying what you already *know* and what you still *want*. Doing this can sometimes be enough to see a way of building a bridge between *know* and *want* ... and so become *unstuck*.

Here are some possible strategies.

- If the question seems too complicated or too general, try simplifying it in some way. For example, break it down into a subset of smaller problems or rewrite it using simpler numbers or easier words.
- If there does not seem to be enough information, list what else you think you need. (Some tasks may deliberately not have enough information included.) Sometimes you may find that you do have the information but it was not in quite the form you expected.

- Tell someone: in trying to explain, you may find that you stress and ignore different parts of the problem and so be able to view it in a new light. Even if there is no one around to help, just saying something out loud to yourself can help considerably – saying it 'in your head' is not as powerful.
- Use the solution if available: you may only need to read a little before you can see what is needed and can continue on your own.
- If you are still stuck, still do not panic: you may need to take a break and do something quite different. Simply freeing your attention can 'unblock' the problem.
- If nothing seems to work, skip over the problem area for the moment. Later studies may help.

The way to make being stuck a more positive experience is to notice not only what helped to get you going again, but also what led you to getting stuck in the first place. This 'learning from experience' is then available to you for use in future situations.

Task 6.13 Ways of working

Think about ways of working on your understanding of a particular topic or type of question.

How might you use worked examples or practice exercises to ensure that you are understanding in a way that will enable you to do similar questions in the more distant future?

Comment
Whenever you encounter a technique or a collection of exercises, consider constructing for yourself:

- a simple question of that type
- a complex or hard question of that type.

Write down which aspects could be changed (the dimensions of variation) and in what ways (the range of change) and still it be basically of the 'same' type.

- If you can manage it, try to express the general 'problem' of that type and, if you cannot actually carry it out in general, at least describe the steps to be used in resolving it.
- Think of each and every technique as a programme for constructing an object that meets certain constraints. Ask yourself what freedom remains, if any, for other solutions.

- Mathematics is learned by doing it.

- Engaging your mental powers in different ways of working can enhance understanding.

- Being 'stuck' can be a positive experience.

- Communicating mathematics clearly and succinctly to yourself and others is an essential element of mathematical study.

7

Using ICT when studying mathematics

This chapter is about the roles that Information and Communication Technology (ICT) can play in doing and learning mathematics; from presenting and demonstrating mathematics work clearly, through calculating, information gathering and various media for learning from instruction to exploration. The chapter is mainly for those who feel less confident about using technology, but also has some pointers and advice for the very confident ICT user. It includes some ideas on using technology to enhance your learning of mathematics.

WHAT IS AVAILABLE

The term Information and Communication Technology (ICT) encompasses both hardware (calculators, computers, input/output devices) and software (programs). Learning outcomes for most university degrees now include at least some element of the use of ICT. It may be for communication, as a presentation or calculating tool, or part of the teaching, learning and assessment strategy.

Technology can be used to:

• reduce the time and tedium of manual calculation, drawing, etc.
• enhance your understanding of mathematics.

The former can be a major help in achieving the latter.

Use this chapter when studying mathematics to give you an awareness of the types of programs available and how to work with them in general. There is little direct instruction in this book on how particular programs work, because not all courses will require you to learn about such programs and those that do will probably provide the means for you to learn how to use them.

The chapter is divided into the sections by the main purpose to which the particular form of ICT is put. 'Learning' has its own section, but using all forms of technology can contribute to your learning.

- Information
- Communication
  - written
  - verbal
  - electronic
- Computation
  - arithmetic
  - algebraic
- Data handling
- Learning
  - instruction
  - practice
  - assessment
  - demonstration/simulation
  - exploration.

Task 7.1 Where are you with ICT?

Think about your previous experiences, if any, of using ICT for:

- doing or learning mathematics
- other purposes.

How do you envisage using ICT for your mathematics studies in the future?

Comment

If you have little or no experience of using ICT, then it will be worth gaining some before starting your studies. In particular, it is worth being able to use the Internet and electronic mail (e-mail), because a great deal of university information is made available through this medium – including information and advice about your university and course. It takes very little time to get the basics, and courses are often available at local colleges or Internet cafés. You may also find that your university offers ICT training.

   If you are already a confident and enthusiastic user of ICT, beware of expanding your knowledge and experience generally at the expense of spending time doing mathematics.

INFORMATION

Encyclopaedic, dictionary and mathematical information is available on CDs or DVDs. However, the biggest range of information is available through the Internet.

The Internet

The Internet or World Wide Web (WWW) is accessed via a browser. Material on the Internet differs from printed material in a number of important ways. The main differences are as follows.

- Scale – in both quantity and breadth. In the matter of breadth, the Internet will provide 'access' to pretty well all the suppliers/magazines/catalogues/journals, many of which are not readily available in the high street. Often you will know the Internet address of interest and you can go there directly.
- Search 'engines' provided on the Internet – typically a very fast way to uncover numerous relevant references: basically, you select the relevant category and key in appropriate words. The system returns a list of Internet addresses and often a brief 'synopsis' of each, so that you can judge their relevance. If there is an overwhelmingly large number of returns, then you can narrow your search.

Intranet

Most universities have websites and mathematics departments have pages of their own. Most of these offer public access to such things as course details, but restricted access to detailed student information. An *intranet* is a site that has restricted access. Every university has such a site and as a student you will be issued with a password enabling you to have access to relevant parts. What is public and what is restricted varies, so it is worth checking even before you get a password.

Mathematical sites

The Internet can provide you with a variety of different kinds of information and resources to support your mathematics learning:

- mathematical language
- mathematicians and the history of mathematics
- mathematics courses
- software and downloadable resources
- interactive sites.

The main problem is that the Internet can absorb a lot of time as you search from one list of sites to another. Perhaps the best place to start is with a guided tour. However, it is important to remember that the Internet changes very quickly and any printed guided tour is likely to go out of date. Therefore, an Internet site with updated live links has been created to support this book.

As you visit websites, it is a good idea to keep a record of the useful sites you find. One effective way to do this is to copy the address from the address bar in your browser and paste it into a MS Word document. The advantage of doing this is that you create live links to the websites within your MS Word document. In order to return to your site, simply click on the address in the MS Word document while you have a live link to the Internet itself.

Task 7.2 A guided tour

Go to http://mcs.open.ac.uk/SkillMath/ and try some of the live links.

You are advised to limit the amount of time you spend on this task to no more than half an hour. Many of the links are 'gateways' to other sites; beware of 'surfing' off too far.

Make brief notes on the contents of each site you visit, including copying the web address (URL) and perhaps give it your own star rating for interest and relevance.

COMMUNICATION

Throughout your course, you will need to communicate mathematics both to yourself and others, not least your tutor. ICT offers means of enhancing such communication in various ways. It enables contact to be made without the necessity of people being in the same place at the same time. It can also facilitate the production of well-presented written work that can incorporate drawings, pictures and graphs.

Electronic

One of the ways of improving your understanding of mathematics, and for getting help when stuck, is to work with other people, including your tutor. It is not always possible to do this face-to-face, but various forms of electronic communication can be used.

Telephone
Talking mathematics without any visual aids may seem challenging. However, speaking carefully and allowing pauses for thought, writing and perhaps the drawing of diagrams, the telephone offers the opportunity for immediate assistance. Some courses provide telephone tutorial opportunities (for example, the Open University Openings courses).

These need to be planned and prepared for in much the same way as any lecture or tutorial. You will need to agree an agenda and ensure that you have appropriate texts to hand.

E-mail and computer conferencing
E-mail and computer conferencing also offer opportunities for collective learning, but have the advantage of not requiring people to be available at the same time. Most universities provide students with an e-mail address for both internal and external use. If this is not true for you, then you can acquire one through one of the many Internet Service Providers (ISPs). An electronic conference is similar to e-mail except that all messages are available to everyone who is entitled to use the conference.

However, there is a slight drawback to using these media – they do not support the use of symbols other than those available on a standard keyboard. This means you need to communicate mathematical problems and solutions in words. (Sometimes, the very act of so doing gives new light in itself.)

It is possible to produce a document in a program capable of rendering mathematical symbols and then attach it electronically to an e-mail or conference message. However, it may not appear on the receiving computer the way it looks on yours, unless that computer has the same programs and fonts available.

Written

Using ICT for producing written mathematical work has both advantages and disadvantages, such as those listed in Table 7.1.

Table 7.1 Advantages and disadvantages of using ICT

Advantages	Disadvantages
Clearer presentation	Can take much longer to produce
Easily duplicated	Can mean learning how to use specialised programs, such as editors
	Electronic media can fail, so multiple back-ups are necessary

Written mathematics can involve the production of text, tables, diagrams and graphs. Most computers are equipped with a suite that includes at least word processing and spreadsheet programs.

Mathematical text
Within ordinary word processors, such as MS Word, there are a number of facilities to aid typing mathematics, for example Equation Editor (which creates a graphic). More advanced mathematical typing can be

done with programs such as Math Type. But for lengthy advanced work, it may be necessary to learn how to use a specialised typesetter such as LaTeX. You will be advised, and offered tuition, if this is necessary for your work.

However, to start with, for many courses you may only need the very basic facilities offered by MS Word, although some of these are not obvious from either the manual or the software's own 'help' facility.

Hints for using MS WORD
1 Put useful tools onto your tool bar.
   To do this, follow the sequence:
   Tools ▶ Customise ▶ Commands ▶
   and drag the icons of your choice to your tool bar (Figure 7.1).
   For instance:

   ▶ Insert

   √α̅   Equation editor

   Ω   Symbol

   ▶ Format

   x^2 Superscript

   x_2 Subscript

Figure 7.1 Customising MS Word commands.

2 Symbols as text.
   Use Insert ▶ Symbol ▶ font ▶ Normal text.

3 You can set up short-cut keys as required, so that the current font can use its own symbols, for example as shown in Table 7.2.

Table 7.2 Symbol short-cut suggestions

ALT	2	3	4	H	R	I	O	0	<	>	+	*	/
Symbol	²	³	$\frac{1}{4}$	$\frac{1}{2}$	√	∫	°	∞	≤	≥	±	×	÷

ALT	A	B	D	E	F	L	M	N	P	S	T
Symbol	α	β	Δ	Σ	φ	λ	μ	ν	π	σ	θ

4 Other useful features include:

- a 'proper' minus sign − (as opposed to -) is available by pressing Ctrl and the ⊟ from the number keypad
- Shift-Ctrl < and Shift-Ctrl > provide dynamic font sizing for highlighted symbols or words
- Ctrl D duplicates a highlighted object.

Tables

Most computers have an 'office' package that includes spreadsheet and word processing programs. Where information needs to be presented in a table, it is possible to use the table facilities in a word processor. Some of these are quite sophisticated and can perform limited calculations. However, a spreadsheet program provides considerably more facilities, including statistical and mathematical functions. Most word processors have the facility to insert a spreadsheet within the text. It is relatively easy and takes very little time to learn how to use a spreadsheet at a sufficient level to take the tedium out of many tasks involving calculations.

About spreadsheets

When you load a spreadsheet program, you will see a grid of *rows* and *columns* forming a series of boxes (*cells*). A cell may contain *text*, a *number* (in various forms) or a *formula* (or nothing). Each cell has its own identity or address: for example, the cell shown with a black border in Figure 7.2 is called B3, i.e. column B row 3.

Much of the power of a spreadsheet derives from being able to link values in one column to those of another by means of formulae. A spreadsheet can be used as a powerful tool for modelling, widely used in industry and commerce, so once you have access to this significant resource, it is worth discovering how else it can support your mathematics learning.

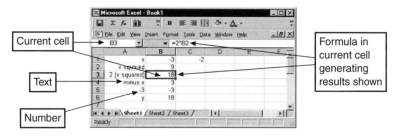

Figure 7.2 Spreadsheet components.

Relative and absolute referencing

One of the big ideas about a spreadsheet is the difference between *relative* and *absolute* referencing. When you use the 'Fill Down' command, the spreadsheet works in a relative way. So when you put B1 = A1*2.5 and use the command 'Fill Down', it automatically calculates in turn: B2 = A2*2.5, B3 = A3*2.5, and so on.

If you want all the calculations to be based on the value in one particular cell, or those from one particular column of cells, then you must use an *absolute* cell reference. This is created in Excel by using the $ sign to 'glue' the part of the reference that is to 'stick' (i.e. not change dynamically).

The following task illustrates this.

Task 7.3 Exploring absolute referencing

The aim of this task is to create a square-shaped multiplication table, up to 12 times 12, using the commands Fill Down and Fill Right to extend a single formula.

B2	=A2*B1

	A	B	C	D	E	F	G	H	I	J	K	L	M
1		1	2	3	4	5	6	7	8	9	10	11	12
2	1	1											
3	2												
4	3												
5	4												
6	5												
7	6												
8	7												
9	8												
10	9												
11	10												
12	11												
13	12												

Starting from cell A2, insert the numbers 1 to 12 in column A. Starting from cell B1, put the numbers 1 to 12 in row 1. Now, in cell B2 enter the formula A2*B1. (In Excel, a formula will always start with '='; other spreadsheets do it differently.)

Note what happens when you fill this formula down from cell B2 to B13 and then fill right from column B to column M. Look at the formula in each of the cells.

Now do the activity again using the formula A2*B1 in the cell B2.

A2 is known as an absolute reference. Look at the resulting formulae. Think about the effect of the absolute referencing.

You might like to also try the formula A$2*B2 in cell B2, before filling down and right as above. Again, look at the resulting formula and think about the effect of putting in the dollar sign ($).

Graphics

Once you have created a table of values, spreadsheet technology enables you to graph them. Inevitably, the first time you do so, it may take longer than creating the graph by hand. But as you become more experienced, creating a graph from a table becomes a very quick task.

Figure 7.3 shows the result of graphing the completed table of values calculated in Excel from the formula generated by $2x^2 - x - 3$. The finished table and graph can then be pasted into a Word document if required.

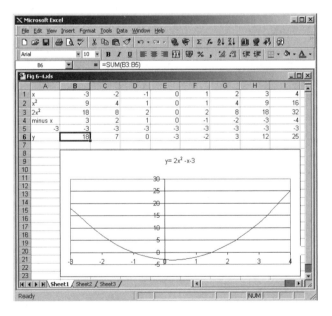

Figure 7.3 Spreadsheet table and graph.

Other graphics, such as simple geometric diagrams, can be produced using facilities in MS Word; for more complicated ones, a drawing or computer-aided design package may be necessary. If you are not familiar with such packages, it is probably a better use of your time to produce diagrams by hand. If your work has to be presented electronically or word processed, you can scan in hand-drawn diagrams.

Presentations

Many courses now require students to make verbal presentations to their fellow students. It can be helpful to have some visual material prepared beforehand, as this saves you having to reproduce complicated material on the board. ICT can provide the means to illustrate such presentations, either by using word processing, etc. (to produce overhead projector slides, OHPs), a computer-based presentation (using, for example, *PowerPoint*) or a suitable mathematics package.

COMPUTATION

Computer technology is digital and early packages did everything with decimals. With increasing computer power, technology is now able to support exact calculation. Together with advanced algebra, you can work with fractions (both numerical and algebraic) in computer algebra systems, as the following example shows. (The illustrations on the next few pages have been produced from hand-held technology.)

These systems can simplify fractions and carry out arithmetic on fractions, giving you a fractional answer automatically rather than a decimal approximation by default (Figure 7.4).

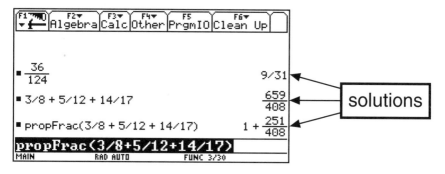

Figure 7.4 Calculation with fractions.

You can also work with algebraic fractions (Figure 7.5).

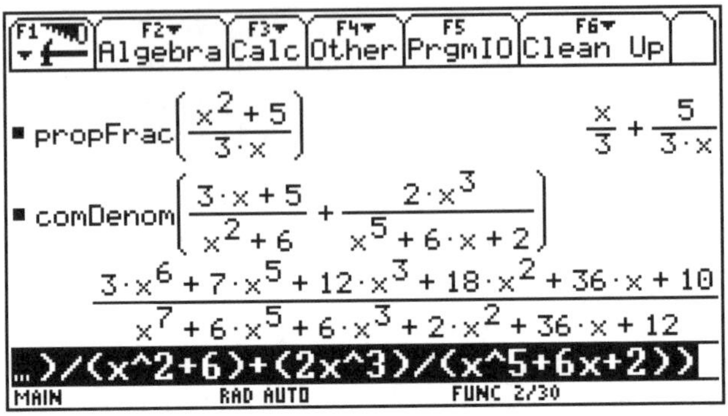

Figure 7.5 Algebraic fractions.

Computer algebra systems

Computer algebra systems (CAS) are available on some hand-held computers. If you are using a computer, you still may not have access to a CAS. If this is the case, you should find out what software, if any, is recommended by your course. It is often possible to buy a student version of the same software or obtain a free 'demo' version.

You can solve equations with CAS (Figure 7.6). The following example illustrates the solution of the pair of simultaneous linear equations $2x - y = -3$ and $-4x - y = -5$. (This might be a problem in algebra involving two unknowns x and y or a problem in geometry asking where the two lines specified by these equations cross.)

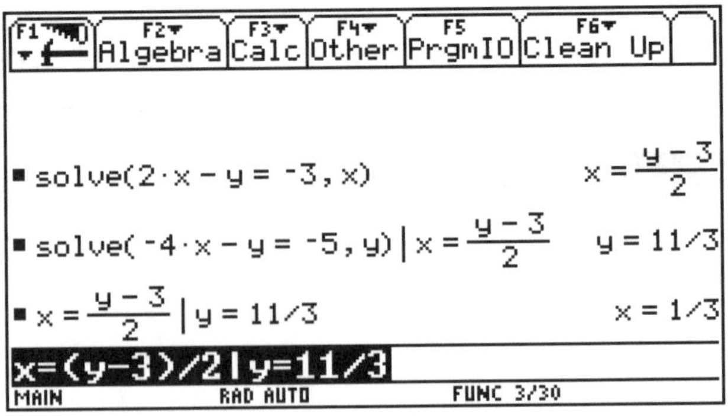

Figure 7.6 CAS system.

The power of CAS becomes more apparent once you see just how much they can do, including calculus (see Figure 7.7) and solving quadratic equations (see Figure 7.8).

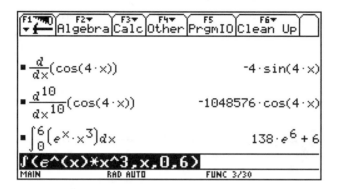

Figure 7.7 Calculus.

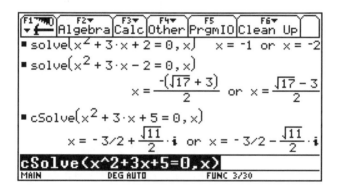

Figure 7.8 Solving quadratic equations.

You should certainly not use CAS to avoid confronting any difficulties you may personally have with algebra; rather, take advantage of the power of the package to explore those aspects you do not yet understand, so as to develop and enhance your understanding. Research evidence shows that CAS can certainly help you enhance your understanding and enable you to discover and develop ideas by algebraic exploration.

CAS can be used to change the order of approach to a topic – so, for example, you could be asked to look at 'real-life' problems involving finding minimum and maximum values *before* you know how to do this algebraically. You could certainly tackle a broader range of problems, where without computer algebra you would be limited to problems involving simpler algebra.

CAS are also useful if you forget how to deal with a topic such as indices (Figure 7.9) or indeed if you have still to find out about them.

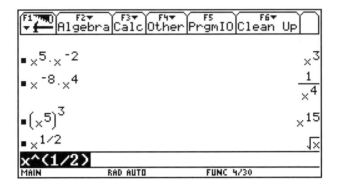

Figure 7.9 Indices.

CAS might also make some of the mathematical techniques taught less important or even redundant and make others necessary. This is part of the power of CAS. The more you use CAS in your learning, the more they can help you to understand a problem and how to solve it.

DATA HANDLING

ICT makes handling large amounts of data feasible. Scientific and technological data can be collected and directly transferred to a computer or calculator using a data logger (see below). Data can be sorted and analysed using data-handling programs such as databases and spreadsheets.

Databases and spreadsheets

Databases and spreadsheets permit complicated statistical formulae to be calculated easily and the results presented as reports including text and graphics. If you are going to be concerned with dealing with data as part of your course, then it is worth learning how to use the sorting and statistical functions available in databases and spreadsheets.

Data logging

An important adjunct to the calculator or the computer is the data logger. (You are most likely to come across a data logger in a laboratory session.) Data loggers come in a variety of guises, but all of them have the following generic facilities.

- Data recording – capturing data you want 'in the field' – either by keyboard entry or by connecting the data logger directly to a measuring instrument. For example, civil engineers take continuous measurements of stress and torque to monitor the adequacy of a structure's current foundations.
- Data upload (or download) to (from) a computer – to enable extensive analysis and graph plotting.

The point about data loggers is that they provide alternate ways of 'capturing' the data to be analysed. Many also include the analytic capabilities required, effectively acting additionally as a calculator. The following example illustrates the use of a CBL2 data logger used in conjunction with a Texas Instruments calculator.

What happens as hot water cools? Clearly, as time goes by, the temperature decreases – but how? Here are two snapshots of an experiment showing a picture of how the water cools down in real time. The x-coordinate is the time in seconds and the y-coordinate records the temperature in degrees Celsius. The calculator stores all the time and temperature data in LISTS and in a STAT PLOT, all ready for display, as shown in Figure 7.10.

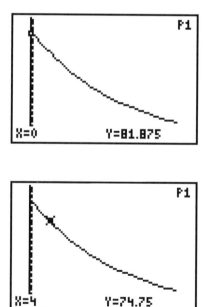

Figure 7.10 Logging temperature fall.

Now, how does the data shape up when compared with the theoretical model – Newton's Law of Cooling, $y = A.B^x + C$? (x and y are as given above, C is the ambient air temperature, which was 24ºC, and A and B are constants.) The values for x and y shown above are used to work out values for A and B, which have been entered into the 'Y =' screen of the calculator (Figure 7.11).

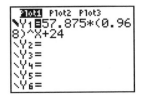

Figure 7.11 Entering Newton's Law.

The trace in Figure 7.12 illustrates how well the theoretical model fits the data. (The thick line is the theoretical curve.)

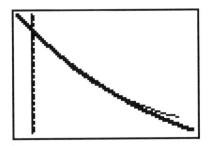

Figure 7.12 Comparing experimental and theoretical results.

The experiment described above was carried out by plugging a temperature probe into a CBL2 data logger. Many other probes are available for use, including a sonic probe to investigate sound patterns and a pulse-rate monitor.

LEARNING

As mentioned earlier, ICT can provide opportunities for various modes and components of teaching and learning:

- instruction
- practice
- assessment
- demonstration/simulation
- exploration.

Role of technology

While learning mathematics, technology offers opportunities for you to:

- acquire new knowledge, skills and understanding
- consolidate skills
- work with graphic images
- explore patterns and relationships
- develop your ability to think logically
- make connections between areas of mathematics that you have learned
- develop mathematical models from realistic data.

Technology can affect how you learn, enabling you to be a more active learner, through:

- experimenting and responding to feedback given by the machine
- experiencing more topics or more examples
- getting deeper into the detail of the mathematics.

You may find it helpful to think of technology as taking one of three roles:

- tutor
- tool
- tutee.

Sometimes, the device is programmed to teach you, sometimes you use it to solve a problem and sometimes you are 'teaching' or programming it to do something new. These roles frequently overlap and sometimes you move between one use and another almost without noticing.

Tutor

There are many examples of programs that have been written to teach you something. They are based on varying views of you as a learner. Individualised learning has its place, but you need to keep in mind the roles of working collaboratively, discussion and problem-solving, when finding an appropriate place for such packages alongside other uses of technology.

Calculus Assistant, shown in Figure 7.13 (overleaf), is an example of a package that has been designed to teach calculus.

Your course may make use of such packages. You will find others available on the Internet. They are, in effect, a series of worked examples that need to be worked on, if understanding is to be developed.

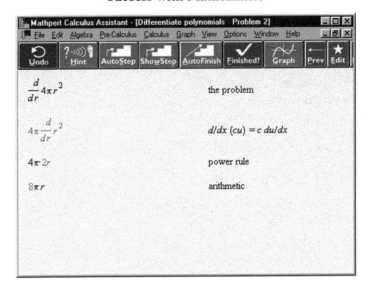

Figure 7.13 Calculus Assistant.

Tools

Liberated, for example, from the tedium of drawing graphs by hand, you can use the technology to build up a library of functions quickly that you come to know really well. Soon you will get a feel for how functions behave and you will find yourself engaged in some exploration – what happens if I change a coefficient here, an index there ...? (This is related to the notion of the 'dimensions of variation' discussed in Chapter 6.)

Multiple representations
Relationships among different types of representations such as tables, equations and graphs are more easily comprehended when several representations are visible. In addition, if they are linked to each other (i.e. when you make a change in one representation, corresponding changes in other representations are offered by the program), several apparently disconnected areas can reinforce one another.

Combinations of representations enable you to explore and identify generalities by experimentation with such questions as these:

- What is the shape of this function?
- What happens when I add (subtract or multiply) these two functions?
- Do the functions $f(x)$ and $g(x)$ have the same value when $x = 0$? If so, what is that value to two decimal places? To three decimal places? (You can ZOOM in to the required degree of accuracy.)

- What does the function look like when I differentiate it? Or integrate it?
- If I move the lines, what then happens to their equations?
- How far do I have to zoom in to find the solution to a pair of simultaneous linear equations to the required degree of accuracy?
- What is the solution algebraically?
- How are the distance or velocity graphs affected by changes in movement?
- How do the algebraic, numerical and graphical versions of a function change as I alter the parameters specifying a given function?

The availability of such capabilities raises some controversial questions about the contemporary learning of mathematics.

Whenever you meet a function for the first time, you can explore it with technology as much as possible to get a real feel for it. When you do feel comfortable with it, you can explore further.

For example, once you get familiar with the graph of $y = \sin(x)$ (when working in degrees) (Figure 7.14), you can move on to investigate graphs of the form $y = a\sin(x)$, where a can be any number, then to $y = \sin(bx)$, where b can be any number, and then to $y = \sin(x) + c$, where c can be any number. Varying these parameters brings about changes to the graph of $y = \sin(x)$ that you started with. You can put these together to start to investigate the three-parameter family of functions specified by the general equation $y = a\sin(bx) + c$. (This is somewhat related to Tasks 6.8 and 6.9 exploring different types of quadratics and cubics under translations and scalings.)

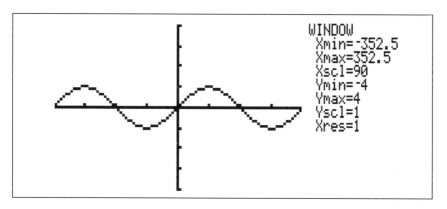

Figure 7.14 $y = \sin(x)$.

Figure 7.15 shows an extension of these ideas, where two members of this family are being added together.

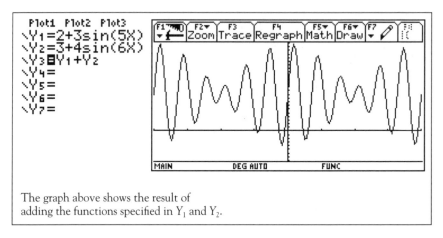

Figure 7.15 Adding two sine functions.

Interactive geometry

Interactive (or *dynamic*) *geometry* is a term used to describe a computer package that allows you to construct and work on geometric objects, to drag them about and to observe what changes and what stays the same.

There are many examples of such packages. These include programs for computer and hand-held technology. Many allow you to draw and measure accurately, for example, points, lines and circles, and to write programs to animate screen diagrams.

Cabri-Géomètre and Geometer's Sketchpad (see Figure 7.16) are two such packages. They can be accessed either on a computer or on a calculator such as the TI-89 or TI-92+. (The calculator version can be downloaded from the Internet, an example of a *flash application*; the computer version can be accessed from the Internet or from a CD.)

What you notice following this continuous movement from particular configuration to particular configuration is that the medians *always* appear to meet at a single point. Would you expect this? This gives you some persuasive evidence that this result could be true for *all* triangles and not just the particular ones drawn (the starting configuration and the other related configurations that it was 'dragged' into). This mathematical result is true in general and can be proved in lots of ways. The point where the medians meet is called the *centroid* of the triangle. (There is lots of information to be found on the Internet by typing the words *median* and *centroid* into a search engine and exploring the sites you find.)

In this very simple example, you can see a triangle.
Lines join each vertex to the mid-point of the opposite side. These lines are called medians. The medians appear to meet at a common point.

By clicking and dragging, the points, you can move triangle around altering size lengths and angles.

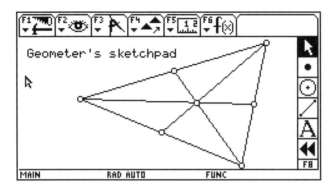

A screenshot from a graphics calculator.

Figure 7.16 An example of interactive geometry.

Task 7.4 Exploring interactive geometry

Using a calculator or a computer version of an interactive geometry package, try creating an equilateral triangle that stays equilateral when you drag any of the corners.

Tutee

The use of logical functions in a spreadsheet can provide a simple introduction to programming. One particularly useful example is 'if-then-else'. The 'if-then-else' structure is a powerful idea in its own right and can enable you to explore some interesting new ideas. Suppose, for example, you want to set up a simulation that involves a probability of 0.3. You can use a formula to enter a random number between 0 and 1 in cell A1. Then in cell B1, you can have 'IF cell A1 is greater than 0.7, THEN make B1 take the value 1, ELSE make B1 take the value 0'.

Programming

It is possible to write programs using a computer or a graphics calculator. This does come with a serious health warning however – writing programs can become addictive and can seriously affect the amount of time you have available for your study! Experimenting with programming is fun and you can write quite simple ones relatively quickly: for example, the program in Figure 7.17 converts pounds to kilograms.

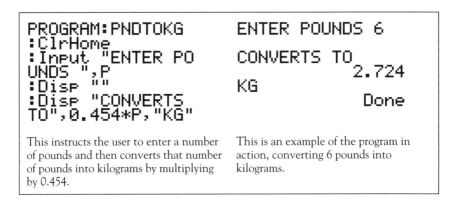

This instructs the user to enter a number of pounds and then converts that number of pounds into kilograms by multiplying by 0.454.

This is an example of the program in action, converting 6 pounds into kilograms.

Figure 7.17 A simple program.

How does technology affect a problem?

In Chapter 6, you were asked to work on some mathematical tasks. Working on such tasks has a new dimension when you have technology. It gives you a new way to express the mathematics.

- The overriding mantra when using technology must be: how has this helped my understanding?

Task 7.5 Problems revisited (for the ICT-confident)

What happens when you use technology to work on 'Quadratic chords' (Task 6.2) rather than pen and paper?

How would you use a computer to work on 'Consecutive products' (Task 6.4) and how would this help?

If you used a dynamic geometry package while working on 'Classifying parallelograms' (Task 6.7), what difference might it make to the problem?

What package would help you to work on a problem such as 'The tethered goat' (Task 6.1)?

Comment
You might start thinking about some of these tasks with pencil and paper if you have not done so already. Once you have formulated the problem in your mind, perhaps with the aid of a mental diagram or table, you could then use a computer package to explore and to do any necessary calculations and measurements.

Cautionary tales: seeing is not always believing
It is a good plan to have some idea of what you expect to see on your graphic calculator or computer screen when you use them to draw graphs. (Chapter 8 has some further examples.)

Task 7.6 What is wrong?

What would a graph of the function $y = \dfrac{10}{4(x-1)}$ look like? (*Hint:* think about what happens, for example, when $x = 1$.)

Look at this calculator output. Are you happy with the graph that the calculator has drawn?

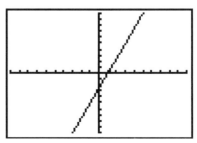

Comment

Well, this certainly should not be a straight line. At $x=1$, the denominator is zero and so the function is undefined at $x=1$; this is no sort of straight-line behaviour.

The calculator is drawing:

$$y=\frac{10}{4} \cdot (x-1) \Rightarrow y=\frac{10}{4}x-\frac{10}{4}, \text{ which } is \text{ the equation of a straight line.}$$

But with brackets round the denominator, $[4(x-1)]$, a quite different picture emerges.

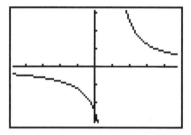 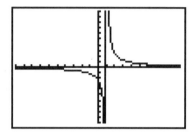

Note: The two graphs above are showing $y=\dfrac{10}{4(x-1)}$, using different scales. The left-hand one is indicating that there is some kind of problem at $x=1$.

Interpret carefully – seeing is not always believing!

REFLECTION

Task 7.7 What next?

Think about your awareness of ICT, and your competence and confidence. Look at the requirements for your course and decide what, if anything, you need to do to improve your knowledge and skills.

- ICT has a role to play in doing, communicating and learning mathematics.
- It needs to be used judiciously: find the appropriate tool and use it reflectively.
- Live links to a range of mathematical sites are at: http://mcs.open.ac.uk/SkillMath/

8

Using calculators

This chapter is about becoming familiar with the calculator you will use in your course and how to use it effectively to support your learning. While it is written for relative beginners, there are ideas and suggestions for further exploration that will be useful for more experienced users. The examples used highlight common errors and misunderstandings.

The chapter is written in two sections. The first section is an introduction to the types of calculators that are available and includes some suggestions for choosing a calculator. The second section is about getting to know your calculator. For the second section, you will need to have a calculator to hand as you work.

You will use your calculator in two distinct ways: to save you time when you already understand the underlying mathematics, and to explore new mathematics, in order to get a better understanding of mathematics you feel unsure about. Both these uses are covered in this chapter.

TYPES OF CALCULATOR

Your course may require that you have a particular type of calculator from a particular manufacturer, so it is important that you find this out before buying one. If you are not restricted, then a good idea would be to consider the advice given here, make your purchase and start to explore it as soon as possible, as it takes some time to become really familiar with a calculator. If you are not required to use a particular type, then it may be useful for you to be aware of different types of calculator, to make it easier for you to share ideas with other students, borrow calculators, and so on.

What is available?

At the simplest level, there are 'non-scientific' or arithmetic calculators. These are usually limited to four operations ($+$, $-$, $\times$, $\div$), but occasionally also have $\sqrt{}$ and % keys. Operations are performed from left to right in the order in which they are keyed in. They are not suitable for a university course.

For any mathematics, science or engineering course, a scientific calculator is the minimum requirement, because operations are performed 'algebraically' (for example, multiplication and division are performed before addition and subtraction). They also have, among other features, trigonometric functions, natural logarithms and π programmed in.

Task 8.1 Order, order

$3 + 4 \times 5 = 23$

Try the following in your head and then on your calculator:

$3 + 4 \times 5$

Did you get what you expected each time?
     Is there anything wrong with the following calculations?

$3 + 4 = 7$ then $7 \times 5 = 35$

So, how did the calculator arrive at the answer 23?
     Which version is correct?

Comment
The calculator is correct. (If your calculator gave the answer 35, then it is an arithmetic calculator and not suitable for a mathematics course.)
     A calculator using algebraic logic will give precedence in a calculation to the following order:

- first, calculations within brackets are performed
- then, powers (indices) are computed
- next, multiplications or divisions are carried out
- finally, additions or subtractions are done.

The convention algebraic logic follows is used to prevent ambiguities in sequence of operations. Using brackets is the way to ensure that the calculations enclosed within them are performed first.

Task 8.2 Dramatic pauses

What is the solution to 10 − 6 − 3?
  What answer does your calculator give?

Comment
As written, the calculation is ambiguous: the answer could be either 7 or 1
depending on whether you read it as:

  10 subtract (pause) 6 subtract 3, i.e. in mathematical notation
  10 − (6 − 3)

or

  10 subtract 6 (pause) subtract 3, i.e. (10 − 6) − 3.

Calculators, unfortunately, are not programmed to interpret dramatic
pauses and changes of voice tone. They will simply calculate according
to the rules with which they have been programmed. In this case, the
calculator carries out the operations from left to right, i.e. the second
interpretation. To force the calculator to compute in a different order, it
is necessary to use brackets.

Scientific calculators

Visually, there are two types of scientific calculator, one with a one- or
two-line screen and one with a larger screen (Figure 8.1). Both types
include built-in trigonometric and statistical functions. The ones with a
large screen can display graphs and are variously referred to as graphics,
graphical graphing calculators or just GCs.

Figure 8.1 Scientific calculators.

GC capabilities are constantly expanding. For example, some GCs have input/output ports and connectors, which allow them to communicate with each other, with computers and with compatible devices such as data loggers and control applications (as illustrated in Chapter 7). Some also have 'Flash ROM', non-volatile memory that enables access to a range of application software. Some models also have built-in computer algebra systems (CAS) and interactive geometry software. Since these machines do so much more than calculate, they are sometimes referred to as *hand-held* or *portable* computers. An example is shown in Figure 8.2.

You should expect to have access to a scientific calculator, with or without graphing capability.

Figure 8.2 Programmable GC showing 3D graphing.

Buying your own calculator

Once you have familiarised yourself with any course or examination regulations, you need to think about factors such as:

- your budget
- your access to computer alternatives to the features of modern hand-held technology
- your ability to read the screen of the calculator and the calculator key labels.

The purchase of a graphics calculator is recommended for anyone studying a mathematics course, as the regular use of one will certainly make all the difference to your understanding and enjoyment of the course. However, learning to use a GC to its full potential takes considerably longer than a non-graphing calculator. (The choice of whether to go for a model with an algebra and/or geometry system on it is yours. These tend to be a bit more expensive. Some examples of their use were illustrated in Chapter 7.)

It may be that you have suitable algebra and geometry packages on a computer that you have regular access to. In that case, you could do most of your work on the computer. However, the portability of the calculator is something you might like to think about. Only some calculators can connect to computers: if this is something you are likely to be interested in, then ensure that the model of calculator you buy has this capability.

For best advice about the current features of individual machines, go to an independent specialist retailer rather than to a general retailer. Also worth noting is that there are separate screens available for some calculators, often used for teaching purposes, that significantly magnify the screen for those who have difficulty in seeing the calculator screen.

GETTING TO KNOW YOUR CALCULATOR

As mentioned above, you should get to know one calculator thoroughly, especially if you are going to take it into examinations. In what follows, you will explore many of the features and built-in functions of your own calculator. Please note that by way of illustration, screen shots have been used in this chapter using graphics calculators, but it is not assumed that you are using one.

To use or not to use your calculator ...

Task 8.3 Arithmetic

For which of the following would you use a calculator?

1 35×150
2 365×435
3 $\sqrt{121}$
4 $\sqrt{3}$
5 $\sqrt{121} \times \sqrt{100}$

Comment
It is your choice, but it is more effective to use your brain in conjunction with your calculator.

Did you use your calculator for $\sqrt{121}$ and $\sqrt{100}$?

Even for the other examples, you should have made an approximation of the order of magnitude of answer you might expect. For example:

35×150; $30 \times 150 = 4500$; $40 \times 150 = 6000$, so expect a solution over 5000.

It is essential to have a rough idea of what a reasonable response from the calculator is, whether a number, a graph or whatever. It is all too easy to make an error when keying in information, so estimating the result first can prevent wasted time or being misled.

> • Use your calculator sensibly: keep up your non-calculator and mental arithmetic skills.

Limitations

Calculators can perform calculations on very large and very small numbers. Most scientific calculators display between eight and ten digits on a single line, so what happens when the answer to a calculation has more than this number of digits?

Task 8.4 All numbers great ...

Work out the following in your head and then do it on your calculator:

   2 million squared (that is 2 million $\times$ 2 million).

Comment

   4 000 000 000 000

But, different scientific calculators show the result in different forms, for example:

   4000000000000

   4E12

   4. ^{12}

These last two are showing the answer in a form of scientific notation. The E stands for exponential. In written scientific notation, this is 4.0×10^{12} (see Task 8.9).

Task 8.5 Larger still

Use your calculator to calculate 2^{1000} (2 to the power 1000, that is $2 \times 2 \times 2 \times 2 \times ...$, a thousand 2s all multiplied together).

On a scientific calculator, use:

2 y^x 1000

On a graphics calculator, use:

2 [^] 1000

Comment

For many calculators, this is beyond their display capacity and so return error messages. For example:

Error

```
ERR:OVERFLOW
1:Quit
2:Goto
```

You need to recognise and accept that all calculators have some limitations and will sometimes return error messages when these limits are reached. It is worth keeping a list of the conditions under which your calculator does this.

'Bugs' and precision errors

You need to be aware that all machines have limitations to numerical data and common functions. For example, calculators use algorithms to calculate functions, but can only store a limited number of decimal places. This means that there can be precision errors due to internal rounding when using fractional and large (> 90) powers.

Key keys

Task 8.6 Subtract?

Look at the two results from two different calculators in Figures 8.3 and 8.4.

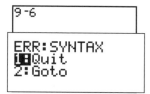

```
9-6

ERR:SYNTAX
1:Quit
2:Goto
```

Figure 8.3 Error message A.

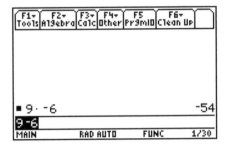

Figure 8.4 Result B.

Why has the first returned an error message and the second an answer of −54?

Comment

The key for the negative sign (directed number) has been used instead of the subtract (operation) key.

In Figure 8.3, the calculator has interpreted the input as the integers 9 and −6 with no operation between them and hence returned an error message. In Figure 8.4, the calculator interpreted the calculation required as 9 times −6.

There are two 'minus' signs on a calculator; one is a directed number (negative), the other an arithmetic operation (subtract). These are entered on a calculator using different keys. The operation key is with the other operation keys and is marked as follows.

$$\boxed{-}$$

The directed number key is indicated differently by different makes of calculator. For example:

$$\boxed{+/-} \qquad \boxed{(-)}$$

Some calculators make the difference in use of the minus sign even more apparent on the display by showing directed numbers with the negative in a higher position than the subtract operation. For example:

9 − ⁻6 meaning '9 subtract negative 6' (equals 15).

Task 8.7 Practice

Practise using the negative and subtract keys on your calculator. Make up a variety of examples and check that the calculator returns the answer you think it should.

Task 8.8 Puzzle

When you multiply two negative numbers you get a positive number. So $-4 \times -4 = 16$.

But what is happening here?

-4^2

-16

Comment

This is another occasion where knowing what sort of answer to expect saves you from making an error. The calculator has worked out:

negative (four squared)

rather than:

(negative four) squared.

(Try saying this aloud and you will find that you need to put the emphasis in different places.)

Putting brackets in will restore your faith in both your mathematics and your calculator.

$(-4)^2$

16

Check whether your calculator needs brackets or not for this calculation.

Task 8.9 Scientific input

Experiment with your calculator – input very large and very small numbers and practise using and interpreting numbers presented in scientific notation. Make notes about what you discover.

You will need to use a particular key, e.g. $\boxed{EE}$ and the $\boxed{+/-}$ or $\boxed{(-)}$ keys. For example,

0.00000007 can be written as 7×10^{-8} and input as $\boxed{7}$ $\boxed{EE}$ $\boxed{(-)}$ $\boxed{8}$

Comment

Using scientific notation in writing or on a calculator is useful when there are lots of zeros involved. It reduces the opportunity for miscounting the number of zeros.

Constants and memory

Almost all calculators have a constant facility, which is very useful and often neglected: unfortunately, they do not all operate with the constant in the same way. The two most common methods of setting up and operating the constant, the 'automatic' and the 'double-press' constant, are described below. Check which way works for your machine. If neither works, track down the calculator's manual and see whether it can be set up by some other means (for example, some calculator constants are based on a key marked $\boxed{\text{K}}$).

Task 8.10 Constant checking

This will enable you to check whether your calculator has an automatic or a double-press constant.

1 Carry out this sequence: $\boxed{2}$ $\boxed{+}$ $\boxed{+}$ $\boxed{=}$ $\boxed{=}$ $\boxed{=}$ ...

2 Carry out this sequence: $\boxed{8}$ $\boxed{+}$ $\boxed{2}$ $\boxed{=}$ $\boxed{=}$ $\boxed{=}$ ...

3 If your calculator has an automatic constant, you will need to discover whether the constant operation is applied to the number *before* the operation each time (i.e. the 8) or the number *after* it (the 2). This needs to be checked out carefully for any new calculator you use, as it varies from model to model. To find out which type you have, carry out the following sequences:

   8 $\boxed{-}$ 2 $\boxed{=}$ $\boxed{=}$ $\boxed{=}$ $\boxed{=}$ ...

   8 $\boxed{\times}$ 2 $\boxed{=}$ $\boxed{=}$ $\boxed{=}$ $\boxed{=}$ ...

   8 $\boxed{\div}$ 2 $\boxed{=}$ $\boxed{=}$ $\boxed{=}$ $\boxed{=}$ ...

Comment
1 For calculators with a double-press constant, this key sequence should produce the 2 times table. (Many calculators show a small 'K' somewhere in the display to indicate that the constant has been activated.) For calculators with an automatic constant, '2' will remain in the display.
2 If successively pressing the equals sign has the effect of changing the number in the display, then you know that your calculator has an automatic constant facility. Such calculators will produce a sequence of numbers. (Other calculators will show '10' on the display throughout.)
3 One problem with the constant facility is that it is rather fragile – it will vanish if any operation key or the 'clear' key is pressed.

It is important that you find out how to use the memory keys on your particular calculator. If you have to use a number several times in calculations, or remember an interim result, then it is a good idea to store it in a memory to save having to key it in every time you want to use it (thus avoiding mis-keying and rounding errors).

Task 8.11 Investigate

Ensure that you are fluent using the memory facilities provided on your calculator.

Rounding

Many people make rounding errors when using a calculator. Basically, you should keep the full accuracy of each result in the calculator (by using memory facilities), rounding only at the very end of the calculation, to a level of precision no greater than that of the original inputs. You should definitely not use a rounded value in a subsequent calculation.

If the final answer to a numerical calculation involves a number with a large number of digits, it is often appropriate to give a rounded answer. Unless the nature of a particular problem determines whether a sensible answer is obtained by rounding down or up, the convention on how to round numbers is as follows.

To round to a given number of *decimal places*:

- look at the digit that is one more place to the right of the desired number of places
- then round up if this digit is 5 or more and down otherwise.

To round to a given number of *significant figures*:

- look at the digit which is that number of places to the right of the first non-zero digit
- then round up if this digit is 5 or more and down otherwise.

Task 8.12 Can you fix it?

What is going on here?

```
1.5+3.2
             5
0.2+0.1
             0
```

Comment

Calculators can be set to show answers to varying numbers of decimal places. The problem here is that the calculator was set to show answers rounded to the nearest whole number.

Note: this facility does not affect the actual calculation within the machine itself, just the displayed answer. You need to know how to set or reset this facility on your calculator: for example, by using the *mode* or *fix* facility.

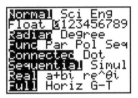

This figure shows a calculator set to return answers to zero decimal places (i.e. to the nearest integer).

To infinity and beyond ...

Task 8.13 Another mystery

Enter the following expression into your calculator: $\dfrac{10-5}{2\sqrt{5}-\sqrt{20}}$
What happens?

Comment

Your calculator should have returned some sort of error message – if it returns a numerical answer, you have probably not entered the quotient correctly. The calculator shown below has returned an answer of 'undef'.

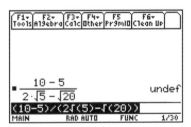

The problem is that the denominator is zero in disguise:

$$\sqrt{20} = \sqrt{4 \times 5} = \sqrt{4} \times \sqrt{5} = 2\sqrt{5} \Rightarrow 2\sqrt{5} - \sqrt{20} = 0$$

and division by zero is something that just cannot be done. Division by zero is said to be undefined.

Fractions

It is interesting to note how little fractions are used now for calculation compared with the days of imperial measures such as inches, when rulers were graduated in eighths, tenths and sixteenths. Nevertheless, an understanding of the manipulation of fractions is very important for algebra and calculus. Many scientific and graphic calculators include a feature that allows calculation with fractions. You can use this feature to check your own understanding of fractions, as well as whenever you need to do a calculation.

Task 8.14 Investigating fractions

Investigate how to enter in a fraction on your own calculator. (Sometimes this is denoted by the ⌐ $a\,^b/_c$ ⌐ key.)

Reciprocals

The reciprocal of a number is defined to be $\dfrac{1}{\text{that number}}$. For example,

the reciprocal of 5 is $\dfrac{1}{5}$ and the reciprocal of $\dfrac{2}{3}$ is $\dfrac{1}{2/3} = \dfrac{3}{2}$. (Use the

fraction facility on your calculator to check that $\dfrac{1}{2/3}$ is $\dfrac{3}{2}$.)

So, given any number x, its reciprocal is $\dfrac{1}{x}$, sometimes written as x^{-1} (which is the notation used on many calculator keypads).

Angles

Have a look at the acute angle shown in Figure 8.5, referred to as $\hat{ABC}$. Can you estimate its size?

You probably wrote something like 40 degrees (or 40° for short). This unit of measurement of angles is an inheritance from ancient Babylonian

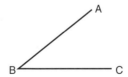

Figure 8.5 An angle.

astronomers. This Babylonian inheritance goes further, in that parts of degrees are measured in minutes (60ths of a degree) and seconds (60ths of a minute), as they are in measuring time. (You will rarely have to consider parts of a degree.)

There may be a feature on your calculator that converts angles expressed in decimal parts of a degree into minutes and seconds. (This key can cunningly and more usefully be used to handle calculations in hours, minutes and seconds without having to do any tedious conversions from, say, decimal parts of an hour to minutes.)

Angles can be given in other, probably less familiar units. The two others implemented on most graphing calculators are called *grads* and *radians*.

Grads can be thought of as a metric measurement of angle, in that there are 100 grads in a right angle (so one grad is slightly less than one degree).

Radians are the choice of those looking at rates of change; this is the mathematician's choice. Your calculator should be in radian mode when working in problems involving trigonometric functions and the calculus unless a problem specifies otherwise. A radian is defined as the angle that subtends at the centre of a circle an arc of the circle's perimeter equal to the radius of the circle (angle AOB in Figure 8.6). Because there are 2π radians in a circle, one radian is a little less than 60 degrees. (In fact, one radian is $180/\pi$ or $57.295\ldots$ degrees.)

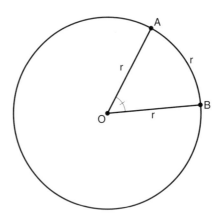

Figure 8.6 Definition of one radian.

You need to ensure that your calculator is set to work in the units you need at the time – degrees or radians.

On a graphics calculator, you should select the appropriate option in the MODE menu (Figure 8.7).

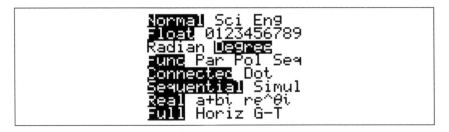

Figure 8.7 Setting angle mode on a graphics calculator.

On a scientific calculator, you need the DRG key. (Keep pressing it to see the letter on the display toggle among Degrees, Radians and Grads.)

Trigonometry

Task 8.15 Sine function

Set your calculator to work in degrees. Press the SIN key and find out whether you need to press the SIN key first and then enter a number, or the other way around. The order does matter and it depends on what type of calculator you are using.

Calculate sin 60°. Can you write the result as a quotient (fraction) that involves the square root of 3?

Comment

sin 60° = cos 30° = 0.8660254 ... and can be written as $\dfrac{\sqrt{3}}{2}$. Numbers written involving square roots are known as *surds*. Because they are exact (and tidier), fractions should be used in preference to decimal alternatives. Unfortunately, most calculators do not display surd forms. It is worth knowing the entries in Table 8.1.

Table 8.1 Key values of trigonometric functions

x	30°	45°	60°
sin (x)	$\dfrac{1}{2}$	$\dfrac{1}{\sqrt{2}}$	$\dfrac{\sqrt{3}}{2}$
cos (x)	$\dfrac{\sqrt{3}}{2}$	$\dfrac{1}{\sqrt{2}}$	$\dfrac{1}{2}$

Random numbers

An interesting feature of modern computers and calculators is their ability to generate pseudo-random numbers. These can be used to simulate situations that have a random component, as shown below.

The random number generator uses a hidden algorithm to generate a number between 0 and 1. Because the algorithm is hidden to you, you can treat the outcome as random. Random number generators are designed to have some basic properties.

- Each outcome can be treated as a randomly chosen number between 0 and 1, independent of the previous outcome.
- Each digit of the result can be thought of as a random choice from the ten digits 0, 1, 2, ..., 9.

Task 8.16 Random

Find the random number generator on your calculator and use it to generate some 'random' numbers.

This is how you might simulate the rolling of a die on a Sharp DAL scientific calculator:

- set up the constant facility ×6
- set the calculator to display 0 decimal places (using fix).

Now each time you press:

| 2nd | | Rand | | = |

you will get an outcome in this virtual die roll.

Task 8.17 It could be you

Repeat this for a constant facility of ×49. What event will this simulate? Can you foresee any problems with this? How might you overcome them?

Easy counting!

Counting problems are among the most perplexing in mathematics, as they are easy to state, but sometimes perilously difficult to solve. For example, what is the smallest number of colours that you need to colour *any* map, so that the colours of any two countries next to each other are different?

How to justify the answer to this baffled mathematicians for over a hundred years. (The result was finally proved in 1976 with the aid of a computer.) So, do not despair if you get stuck – sometimes ideas in mathematics take a little time to become 'obvious' and this is true no matter what stage in mathematics you might be at.

There are three keys on your calculator that are useful for solving counting problems. The first is:

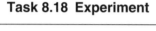 (or $\boxed{x!}$) pronounced as n (or x) factorial.

Task 8.18 Experiment

Experiment with your calculator to see what this key does …

Comment
The numbers get very large very quickly, as shown below.

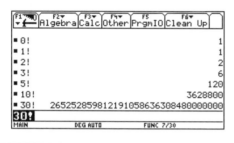

How does this fit into the idea of a counting problem?

How many ways can you arrange the three letters S, U, M?

There are three ways to pick the first letter – S, U or M.

For each of these ways, there are two ways to pick the second letter.

SU	UM	MS
SM	US	MU

For each of these ways, there is only one way to pick the third letter.

SUM	UMS	MSU
SMU	USM	MUS

So, there are $3 \times 2 \times 1 = 6$ ways to arrange the three letters. Can you see a connection between this and the work you did on factorial numbers? It turns out that $3! = 3 \times 2 \times 1 = 6$ and that in general:

$$n! = 1 \times 2 \times 3 \times \ldots \times n$$

By a similar argument to the one above, if you have any number of distinct objects, n, you can arrange them in $n!$ ways.

The other two keys for counting problems are $\boxed{\text{nPr}}$ and $\boxed{\text{nCr}}$. An understanding of how to use these and situations in which you might use them will certainly give you food for thought (see Tables 8.2 and 8.3).

Table 8.2 Permutations

Key	Where to use it?	Explanation and answer
P stands for permutation	If there are 8 people in a race, in how many ways can the first, second and third positions be given?	This question is asking, 'How many ways are there to choose 3 things from 8 where order matters?'
	In how many ways can a chairperson, a treasurer, a secretary and an entertainment convenor be chosen from a maths club having 25 members?	$8\ \text{nPr}\ 3 = 336$ This is asking exactly the same type of question as the first one, 'In how many ways can we choose 4 things from 25 where order matters?' $25\ \text{nPr}\ 4 = 303600$

(Permutations are like picking prize winners – position is paramount.)

Table 8.3 Combinations

Key	Where to use it?	Explanation and answer
C stands for combinations	There are 20 people at a party. In how many ways can you choose 4 people to tidy up?	This question is asking, 'How many ways are there to choose 4 things from 20 where order does not matter?'
	Can you see that this problem is different from the one above. The 4 people tidying up do not have labels attached like 'chief cook and bottle washer' – they are all on an equal footing	$20\ \text{nCr}\ 4 = 4845$

(Combinations are like choosing choristers – only competition is considered.)

You can go a very long way in mathematics by spotting that some problems are essentially the same as problems that you have already done, i.e. seeing the general in the particular (as discussed in Chapter 6).

- Become familiar with the calculator you use for examinations and be aware of other types of calculator.

- Do not be fooled by the foibles of your calculator – think about the type of answer to expect.

- Use your experiences with the calculator as a taster of the mathematics to come. Get some idea of the nature of studying mathematics.

- Feel confident to explore and enjoy.

9

What next?

This chapter is about the next steps you need to take to prepare yourself for starting a mathematics course. It reiterates the main points from the rest of the book, so that you can reflect on your own situation and decide what you now need to do and how to make the best use of the time you have remaining before starting your course.

INTRODUCTION

Every year, a number of students have the disappointment of not completing a course successfully. Some of the reasons for this are unavoidable, such as sudden illness, accident or family crisis; but the main reasons are related to not being properly prepared for the experience of studying at university.

Many students find the first year of university study to be a very difficult time. This can be due to problems that are academic, domestic, social, financial or a combination of these. Research has shown that the students most likely to have problems so severe as to cause them to drop out are those who come from families with no history of attending university and whose academic qualifications are limited. If this is your situation, then your preparation needs to be extra thorough and when you start your course make sure you ask anything of which you are uncertain. That way you will be one of the many in your situation who succeed in their chosen course of study.

This book is about the study skills you need to develop and some of the arrangements you need to make. At the beginning, it was suggested that you should make notes or mark those sections needing your attention.

Task 9.1 Things to do

Look back through your notes or the sections you marked and list the things you still need to do or to work on. Perhaps put them in some order of priority with an estimate of time to do and a target date for completion.

Comment
If you did not make notes, then now is the time to skim through the book and make notes for the particular purpose of deciding what you need to do next. However, although this book has mainly concentrated on study skills and techniques, there are other issues to consider too.

DOMESTIC PREPARATION

To be properly prepared for a course of study involves both academic and domestic preparation. If not organised sufficiently ahead of time, domestic issues can impinge on actual course time.

Task 9.2 Living arrangements

What changes will there be to your domestic arrangements? How might you prepare so that domestic problems do not detract from your academic studies?

Comment
Most domestic problems are easily solved with enough money but the problem for many university students is that financing their studies is a huge problem on its own.

You will need to ensure you have the right resources organised, including time (see Chapter 2).

If taking a university course involves you moving from home for the first time, you will need to consider such things as:

- where to live
- transport to and from university if not on campus
- food preparation (canteen and ready meals are expensive: perhaps make sure you can cook cheap nutritional meals)
- financial arrangements (banking, budgets, loans, etc.)
- laundry (where and how)
- communication with family and friends (phone cards, a mobile phone, etc.).

ACADEMIC PREPARATION

Academic preparation comprises ensuring you have the skills, knowledge and mental preparation for your course. Part of this is the study skills you have been developing while working through this book. It also includes any ICT knowledge and skill that you need.

However, there are two other elements. One is ensuring that you are mathematically 'fit' (your mathematical knowledge and understanding is sufficient for the course you are taking and that you are 'in practice'); the other is that you have some understanding about how mathematicians think and work (you are going to be taught by them). One way to bring this about is to read about both mathematics and mathematicians.

Mathematics

Most university courses have prerequisite qualifications for each course and normally you will not have been accepted for the course without them. (The Open University does not have such prerequisites for undergraduate courses, but does indicate the level of knowledge that will be assumed.) Most university mathematics departments assume that you are fluent in the use of this prerequisite mathematics. Even the few months between finishing an A-level course and starting a university course can be sufficient for you to lose some fluency unless practice is maintained: the longer the gap, the more important it is to regain mathematical 'fitness'.

Practice
Use the work from your last mathematics course and redo a few examples of each topic relevant to your university course. Do not do all the examples, just sufficient to remind you of the process – and build up your fluency, understanding and confidence.

Remember the strategy suggested in Chapter 6.

Whenever you encounter a technique or a collection of exercises, consider constructing for yourself:

- a simple question of that type
- a complex or hard question of that type.

Write down which aspects could be changed (the dimensions of variation) and in what ways (the range of change) and still it be basically of the 'same' type.

- If you can manage it, try to express the general 'problem' of that type and, if you cannot actually carry it out in general, at least describe the steps to be used in resolving it.
- Think of each and every technique as a programme for constructing an object that meets certain constraints. Ask yourself what freedom remains, if any, for other solutions.

Improving your understanding

If you find topics that you realise you do not fully understand, then you may need to borrow or acquire a textbook or find help on the Internet. (See the list of resources at the end of this chapter.)

Background reading

When you start your course you are going to be lectured and/or tutored by mathematicians. It is worth getting into the way that they think by reading books on and about mathematics and mathematicians. If this is something you have not done before, then start with the more 'popular', less dense texts written for general consumption before working onto some of the more dense 'standard' works.

RESOURCES

The main resource list for this book is maintained on http://mcs.open.ac.uk/SkillMath/ – this has live web links to a variety of sources and gateways to many more.

The following is a list of books that you might find useful to buy or borrow from a library (some may be out of print). Be selective, but try to find ones that challenge your mathematical thinking.

Mathematics revision

Graham, L. and Sargent, D. (1981) *Countdown to Mathematics*, Vols 1 and 2, Addison-Wesley Publishers Ltd in association with Open University Press, Wokingham. (Volume 1 – arithmetic, simple algebra, graphs, representing data; Volume 2 – algebra, trigonometry.)

There are plenty of other mathematics textbooks around; look in book-shops and libraries until you find one that suits your needs (maybe lots of practice exercises at your level and beyond, perhaps offering straight-forward or multiple explanations). Some revision guides can be succinct yet informative enough to refresh your understanding.

Mathematics reference

Dictionaries

There are several mathematical dictionaries available. Some are more technical, giving definitions in symbols and words, whereas others give explanations in words and include short biographies of mathematicians. Choose one that suits you.

Wider mathematical reading

Popular texts

Doxiadis, Apostolos (2000) *Uncle Petros and Goldbach's Conjecture*, London, Faber & Faber.

Though this is a work of fiction, it is a story of the search for a solution to a famous problem and of the possible pitfalls in a research project that is too restricted in its outlook. There is a mix of humour, pathos and mathematics.

Flannery, S. (2000) *In Code: A Mathematical Journey*, London, Profile Books.

This is a book about growing up in a mathematical household written when Sarah was a teenager. It includes some problems with solutions and explanations.

Peterson, I. (2001) *The Mathematical Tourist: New and Updated Snapshots of Modern Mathematics*, W. H. Freeman, Basingstoke, Palgrave.
Singh, S. (1998) *Fermat's Last Theorem*, London, Fourth Estate.

An account of Andrew Wiles' proof of Fermat's Last Theorem, but it touches on many of the problems that have interested mathematicians over the centuries.

Singh, S. (2000) *The Code Book*, London, Fourth Estate.

A history of codes and ciphers and their modern applications in Internet security.

Stewart, I. (1997) *Does God Play Dice?* London, Penguin.

An introduction to the field of chaos, it gives an insight into the mathematics behind fractals as well as many other situations where you can find chaotic behaviour.

Stewart, I. (1998) *The Magical Maze: Seeing the World Through Mathematical Eyes*, London, Orion Paperback.
Stewart, I. (1998) *Nature's Numbers: Discovering Order and Pattern in the Universe*, London, Orion Paperback.
Stewart, I. (1996) *From Here to Infinity*, Oxford, Oxford University Press.

An introduction to how mathematics is developing today, it shows how many ideas, old and new, can be important in answering questions in today's world.

Barrow, J. D. (1993) *Pi in the Sky: Counting, Thinking and Being*, London, Penguin.

The author discusses rival views of where maths comes from and how it is done.

Guillen, M. (1995) *Five Equations That Changed the World*, London, Abacus.

Tells the stories of five of the most important mathematicians and scientists in history and gives the background to their discoveries of 'world changing' equations.

More challenging texts
Simmons, G. F. (1991) *Calculus Gems: Brief Lives and Memorable Mathematics*, Berkshire, McGraw-Hill.

This book includes brief lives of 33 important mathematicians. They are followed by 26 notes on significant moments in maths, from Pythagoras' theorem to rocket propulsion.

Courant, R. and Robbins, H. (revised by Ian Stewart) (1996) *What is Mathematics?* Oxford, Oxford University Press.

This is a classic book, covering a broad spectrum of fundamental mathematical ideas. It has been updated to describe mathematical developments such as the proof of the Four Colour Theorem and Fermat's Last Theorem.

Study skills

Kahn. P. (2001) *Studying Mathematics and its Applications*, Basingstoke, Palgrave.

Advice on how to study and apply complex mathematical ideas with exercises and extension material.

Northedge, A., Thomas, J. and Peasgood, A. (1997) *The Sciences Good Study Guide*, Milton Keynes, The Open University.

A study guide for students of science, technology and engineering with a basic (sub A-level) mathematics help section.

Cottrell. S. (1999) *The Study Skills Handbook*, Basingstoke and London, Macmillan Press Ltd.

A general guide to study skills with useful checklists.

Good luck with your studies. Enjoy the mathematics.

Index

absolute referencing 129–30
abstraction 10–11
academic preparation 166–7
access courses 3
active learning 1–2, 25; course units 35–6; lectures 27; reading 37–8; tutorials 28; *see also* learning; studying
addresses: Internet 125; spreadsheet cells 128
advice *see* help and support
alcohol, effects 18
algebra: computers 132–4; fractions 132; prerequisite 5; problem solving approach 104
algebraic logic 146
allocation, marks 54–5
ambiguities, symbols 87
angles, calculators 157–9
annotation, handbooks 62, 66–7
anxiety 18, 73–4
approaches: doing mathematics 98–121; learning 23–4; *see also* problem solving; strategies
approximate answers 149
arithmetic calculators 146
assertions 106, 118–19
assessment 42–75; assignments 43–58; examinations 58–75
assessment-feedback cycle 44
assignments 43–58; checklists 47, 52–3, 56; feedback 43–4, 56–7; incomplete 53–4; key words 49; marks and marking 44–5, 53–8; notes 33; planning 46–8; presentation 51–3; resources 50–1; strategies 47–8
association, learning technique 23–4
attendance, lectures 26

audience: assignments 51; explanations 114; presentations 83; projects 86; written material 84–5
audio-visual resources 16, 33
axes 89–91

background reading 167–9
books: notes 31–2, 37–8; sources 17; suggested titles 167–9; textbooks 37–40; *see also* reading
brackets: calculators 146–7, 153; written mathematics 87
brain, learning 23
breathing exercises 74
buying calculators 148–9

Cabri-Géomètre 140
calculations, spreadsheets 128
calculators 15, 145–63; angles 157–9; brackets 146–7, 153; buying 148–9; constant functions 154; decimal places 155–6; directed numbers 152; error messages 151–2; estimated results 143, 149; examinations 67; fractions 157; graph plotters 93; interactive geometry 140; large numbers 150–1; random numbers 160; reciprocals 157; scientific notation 150, 153; time 158; trigonometry 159; types 145–9; *see also* Information and Communication Technology
calculus, computers 133
Calculus Assistant 137–8
calendar *see* timetables
Cartesian coordinates 91–2
CAS *see* computer algebra systems
categorising *see* characterising

cells, spreadsheets 128
centroids 140–1
change, dimensions of variation 113
characterising 107–12, 113
checklists: assignments 47, 52–3, 56;
    examinations 69–70
classifying *see* characterising
combinations 162
communication: calculators 148; diagrams
    88–9; expressing oneself 117–19; fellow
    students 50; graphs 89–97; ICT 125–31;
    learning technique 114–16;
    mathematical 52, 76–97; reading 80–2;
    representations 76–80; speaking 82–4;
    symbols 76–9, 85, 87; teaching staff 20
complex numbers 31–2
computation, ICT 131–4
computer algebra systems (CAS) 132–4
computer conferencing 126
computer-marked assignments 45
computers 15–16; calculator alternative
    148–9; diagrams 88–9; drawing features
    88–9; learning packages 33; portable
    148; presentation images 84; word
    processors 88; *see also* Information and
    Communication Technology
condensing notes 65
confidence 74
conjectures 106, 114–16
connecting words 85
constant functions, calculators 154
constraints 114
constructive activity 99, 114
content: school mathematics 3–4;
    university mathematics 10–11
continuous assessment *see* assignments
convincing process 106, 117–19
coordinates 91–2
copying 51, 53
counting problems 160–2
courses 3–5; advice 58; calculator
    requirements 145–6; Internet 124;
    mapping 65; preparation 7–21; units
    35–6
coursework *see* assignments
creativity 114
cubics 111–12, 115
customising, MS Word 127–8

data: handling 134–6; loggers 134–6;
    representation 89–91
databases 134
deadlines 46–7
decimal places 155–6

degrees 157–9
dependent variables 90–1
development: mathematical
    communication 118; understanding 120
diagonals 108–9
diagrams 76–9, 88–9; assignments 53;
    conviction aid 117; ICT 131; notes 38;
    problem solving 100
diary, learning experiences 8, 34–5
difficulties: being 'stuck' 119–20; personal
    53, 71
dimensions of variation 105–6, 113,
    116–17, 120
directed numbers 152
discussions, preparation 82–3
distance-learning: course units 35–6;
    information sources 22; notes 30–1;
    schedule 25; tutors 20
doing/undoing 112–13
domestic preparation 165
drawing features, word processors 88
dropping out 164
dynamic geometry 140–1

e-mail 123, 126
ECA *see* end-of-course assessment
electronic assignment submission 45, 52
electronic communication 125–6
end-of-course assessment (ECA) 46
energy levels 18–19
engagement *see* active learning
environment, study 14–15
equals sign 85
Equation Editor 126–7
equation solving 132
equipment 15–16, 69
equivalence 85
errors: calculators 151–2; marking 58
estimation: calculator answers 143, 149;
    task durations 25
examinations 58–75; during 72–4; format
    62–3; materials 69; mock 68; past papers
    62, 67–8; planning answers 72–3;
    preparation 70–1; purpose 58–9;
    questions 63, 68–9; unexpected
    problems 71; *see also* revision
examples 37; *see also* exercises
exercises 10; constructing 120; course
    preparation 166–7; generalising 120;
    textbooks 38; *see also* problem solving;
    questions
expectations, universities 4–5, 166
experimental results 135–6
experimentation *see* investigations

explanations 117–19
exploration *see* investigations
exponential form 150, 153
expressing oneself 100–1, 117–19
extrapolation 93

factorial 161–2
families 19–20
fear, speaking 82
feedback 43–4, 56–7; *see also* reflection
fellow students: critical readers 118;
    learning resource 50; revision 66; self-
    help groups 29
fitness: mathematical 166; physical 18
flow charts 88–9
fluency, mathematical techniques 166
formal assessment 44–6
format, examinations 62–3
formative assessment 42
formulae: examinations 62; spreadsheets
    128
foundation courses 3
fractions 131–2, 157
freedom and constraint 101, 114
friends 19–20
full-time study 11, 14, 24–5
functions: cubics 111–12, 115; graphical
    representation 91–7; quadratics 96–7,
    101–2, 110–11, 115; representations
    138–40; table 92–3

GCs *see* graphics calculators
generalising: learning technique 23;
    problems 116–17; solutions 102–6, 107
Geometer's Sketchpad 140–1
geometry, interactive 140–1
gradients 94–5
grads 158
grammar 85
graphics, ICT 130–1
graphics calculators (GCs) 147–8
graphs 89–97; calculators 143; cubics
    111–12, 115; data representation 89–91;
    mathematical functions 91–7;
    quadratics 96–7, 101–2, 110–11, 115;
    spreadsheets 130
group study 25–9, 45–6
guidelines, written mathematics 84–7

hand-held computers 132, 148
handbooks 62, 66–7
handwriting 69, 87
help and support: assignments 50–1;
    course units 36; people 19–20; self-help

groups 29, 66; teaching staff 20, 36;
    universities 10
home arrangements 14–15, 165
horizontal axis 89–91

i 31–2
ICT *see* Information and Communication
    Technology
ideas: communications 76–80; expressing
    100–1; investigating 37
if and only if 85, 107
iff *see* if and only if
illness, examinations 71
images *see* diagrams; graphs
imagination, problem solving 99–102
implies sign 85
independent variables 90–1
indices 134
individualised learning 137–8
information: background 168–9; Internet
    124–5; problems 119; sources 22; *see
    also* resources
Information and Communication
    Technology (ICT) 122–44;
    communication 125–31; computation
    131–4; data handling 134–6;
    information 124–5; Internet 17, 123–5,
    167; learning 136–44; presentations 84;
    see also calculators; computers; software
interactive geometry 140–1
intercepts 94–5
Internet 17, 123, 124–5, 167
interpolation 93
interpretation, mathematical writing 81
intranet 124
invariance 113
investigations: algebra 133; functions
    138–9; new ideas 37
involvement, family and friends 19–20

journal 8, 34–5
justification, assertions 106, 118–19

key words 49, 68–9

labels 53, 88
language: mathematics 76; process words
    49, 68–9; word meanings 113
layout, assignments 52
learning 98–121; assessment-feedback
    cycle 44; by communicating 114–16;
    experience 120; ICT 136–44;
    individualised 137–8; journal 8, 34–5;
    techniques 23–4, 114–16; *see also* active

learning; distance-learning; studying; understanding
lecturers, assignment advice 51
lectures 26–7, 29–30
legibility 87
leisure 18
limitations: calculators 151; word meanings 113
linear functions 94–5
living arrangements 165

magnification, calculator screen 149
management, time 11–14, 72–3
mapping, course content 65
marks and marking: assignments 44–5, 53–8; errors 58; examinations 75
materials, examinations 69
mathematical gems 33–4
meanings, mathematical 113
medians 140–1
memories 155
mental powers 99–112; characterising 107–12; conjecturing and convincing 106; expressing ideas 100–1; imagining 99–100; organising 107–12; specialising and generalising 102–6
methods: book usage 5–6; study 22–41
minus sign 128, 152
mock examinations 68
modules, notes 30–1
motivation 8–9, 19
MS Word 88, 126–8; see also word processors

n! 161
negative feelings 74
negative sign 128, 152
notation 84, 86–7
notes 29–35; assignment preparation 33; audio-visual materials 33; computer packages 33; condensing 65; course units 35–6; diagrams and sketches 38; lectures 26, 27, 29–30; problem solving 100–1; revision 33; storage 16; study modules 30–1; textbooks 31–2, 37–8

objectives, assignment questions 54
objects: characterising 107–12; freedom and constraints 114, 120
online resources 17
operations, calculators 146–7
order, arithmetic operations 146–7
organising: problem solving 107–12; resources 14–17

origin, graphs 89
overflow, calculators 151

parabolas see quadratic functions
parallelograms 108–9
parameters, functions 139–40
participation 27, 28
past papers: learning resource 10; revision resource 62, 67–8
people: learning resource 51; relationships 18–20; see also fellow students; tutors
performance, examinations 59
permutations 162
plagiarism 51
planning: assignments 46–8; examination answers 72–3; revision 59–61; time 12–13
plotting graphs 91–3
portable computers 148
portfolios 46
positive feelings 74
practice exercises see exercises
precision errors, calculators 151
preparation: academic 166–7; assignments 33; course units 35; domestic 165; examinations 62–3, 70–1; lectures 26; presentations 83–4; projects 86–7; tutorials 28, 82–3; university study 2–3, 7–21
preparatory assignments 45
prerequisites, universities 4–5, 166
presentation (written work) 51–3, 126
presentations 83–4, 131
pressure 59
priorities 13–14
private study 24–5; course units 35–6; textbooks 37–40
problem solving: approaches 49–50, 104; characterising 107–12; conjecturing and convincing 106–7; initial steps 100–1; knowing and wanting 100–1; scope of variation 105–6; specialising and generalising 102–6; when 'stuck' 109; see also strategies
problems: consecutive products 103–4, 106, 107; quadratic chords 101–2; tethered goat 99–100, 105; see also difficulties; exercises
process words 49, 68–9
products, consecutive numbers 103–4, 106, 107
programming 141–2
projects 46, 86–7
proofs 85–6, 106, 118–19

properties, objects 108–9, 113, 114
purchasing calculators 148–9
Pythagoras' theorem 77–8

quadratic equations 13, 77–8
quadratic functions 96–7, 110–11; chords
    101–2; tangents 115
questions: assignments 49, 54–5;
    examinations 63, 68–9, 72–3;
    generalising 120; key words 49; lectures
    27; reading 55; tutorials 28; see also
    exercises; problem solving
quotations 51

radians 158
random numbers 160
rational numbers 77–8
reading 35–40; background 167–9;
    mathematics 80–2; skimming 6; see also
    books
reasons, mathematics study 8–9
reciprocals 157
reference texts 167
referencing, spreadsheets 129–30
reflection: study sessions 36; studying 8;
    tutorials 28; see also feedback
relationships: mathematical 113, 114;
    personal 19–20
relative referencing 129–30
relaxation techniques 73–4
remainders 102
representations 76–80, 138–40
requirements: calculators 145–6;
    universities 4–5, 166
resources: books 17; equipment 15–16;
    Internet 17, 124–5, 167; organisation
    14–17; preparation 165; problem
    solving 50–1; reference texts 167;
    revision 62, 167; study skills 169; study
    space 14–15; see also people; time
responsibilities 18–19
revision 59–68; course preparation 166–7;
    last-minute 68; notes 33; planning
    59–61; resources 62; self-help groups 29,
    66; techniques 62–8
rigour 11
rough answers 149
rounding 151, 155–6

scales, graphs 91
schedules 25; see also timetables
school mathematics 4
scientific calculators 146–8
scientific notation 150, 153

screens, calculators 148–9
search engines 124
selective reading 38–9
self-assessment 42
self-care 18
self-help groups 29, 66
self-talk 74
seminars see tutorials
short-cuts, MS Word 128
shorthand, mathematical see symbols
significant figures 155
simplification, problems 119
sine functions 139–40
sketches 38, 93–7
skim reading 6, 39
software: calculators 148; computer
    algebra systems 132–4; data handling
    134–6; interactive geometry 140–1;
    mathematical typing 126–7; multiple
    function representation 138–9;
    spreadsheets 128–30, 134; teaching
    packages 137–8; word processors 88,
    126–8
sources, information 22
speaking 82–4; convincing process 117;
    when 'stuck' 120
specialising: learning technique 23;
    problem solving 101, 102–6, 107
specimen papers 62
spreadsheets 128–30; data handling 134;
    logical functions 141
starting points, problem solving 100–1
stationery 15
statistical functions 147
statistical graphs 89
storage 16
strategies: assignments 47–8; checking
    understanding 36; concentration 36;
    doing mathematics 40; examinations
    72–3; learning journal 34; lectures 27;
    reading mathematics 81; study
    environment 14–15; time management
    11–14; when 'stuck' 119–20; see also
    problem solving
stress 18, 71
stuck, strategies for getting 'unstuck' 119
students 3; see also fellow students
study partners 20
study skills 24, 169; see also learning;
    problem solving; strategies
studying 22–41; diary 8, 34–5; effectively
    11, 13; environment 14–15; modes
    22–4; notes 29–35; with others 25–9;
    places 14–15, 25; preparation 2–3,

165–7; reading 35–40; stages 8; on your
own 24–5
submission, assignments 44–6, 52–3, 56
subtraction, calculators 147, 151–2
summaries, revision technique 65–6
summative assessment 42
supervisions *see* tutorials
support *see* help and support
surds 159
symbols 76–9; ambiguities 87; e-mail 126;
MS Word 127–8; use 85

table facilities, ICT 128
talking *see* speaking
tangents 115
teaching: learning technique 114–16;
packages 137–8; revision technique 66;
universities 10–11
teamwork, group assignments 45–6
techniques: learning 23–4, 114–16;
relaxation 73–4; revision 62–8; *see also*
strategies
technology *see* Information and
Communication Technology
telephone communication 125–6
tension 73–4
tethered goat problem 99–100, 105
textbooks 31–2, 37–40; *see also* books
themes, mathematical 99, 112–14
theorems 38, 106–7
thinking mathematically 98–9
time: calculators 158; graphs 89–90;
management 11–14, 72–3; study periods
25
time-filling 13
timetables 24–5; assignments 46–7;
revision 60–1; study 12
titles, diagrams 88–9
tool bars, MS Word 127
tools, ICT 138–41
triangles 140

trigonometric functions 139–40, 146–7,
159
tuition, universities 10
turning points 97
tutor-marked assignments 44–5
tutorials 27–8; revision 66; speaking up
82–3; telephone 125–6
tutors, help and support 20, 36, 51, 56–7
typing 87, 126–7

understanding 116–17; checking 36;
developing 120; improving 167; lecture
material 26–7
units 53
universities: expectations 4–5, 166;
mathematics teaching 10–11; websites
124

variables: axes 89–91; italics 88; letter
choice 86–7
variation, dimensions 105–6, 113, 116–17,
120
vertical axis 89–91
visual aids 83–4
visualisations *see* diagrams; graphs

websites *see* Internet
word processors 88, 126–8
working hours: employment 18; study
11–12, 14, 24–5
working places 14–15, 25
workings 55–6
workshops *see* tutorials
World Wide Web (WWW) *see* Internet
writing: handwriting 69, 87; mathematics
84–8
writing up notes 30
written material, ICT 126–31
WWW (World Wide Web) *see* Internet

$y = mx+c$ 94–5